THE

PEDAGOGICAL WALLPAPER

PETER LANG
New York • Washington, D.C./Baltimore • Bern
Frankfurt am Main • Berlin • Brussels • Vienna • Oxford

THE PEDAGOGICAL WALLPAPER

Teaching Charlotte Perkins Gilman's "The Yellow Wall-paper"

EDITED BY
Jeffrey Andrew Weinstock

PETER LANG
New York • Washington, D.C./Baltimore • Bern
Frankfurt am Main • Berlin • Brussels • Vienna • Oxford

Library of Congress Cataloging-in-Publication Data

The pedagogical wallpaper: teaching Charlotte Perkins Gilman's
"The yellow wall-paper" / edited by Jeffrey Andrew Weinstock.
p. cm.
Includes bibliographical references and index.
1. Gilman, Charlotte Perkins, 1860–1935. Yellow wallpaper.
2. Gilman, Charlotte Perkins, 1860–1935—Study and teaching. 3. Feminism and literature—United States. 4. Mentally ill women in literature. 5. Married women in literature. 6. Sex role in literature. I. Weinstock, Jeffrey Andrew.
PS1744.G57 Y4533 813'.4—dc21 2002073038
ISBN 0-8204-6305-1

Die Deutsche Bibliothek-CIP-Einheitsaufnahme

The pedagogical wallpaper: teaching Charlotte Perkins Gilman's
"The yellow wall-paper" / ed. by Jeffrey Andrew Weinstock.
–New York; Washington, D.C./Baltimore; Bern;
Frankfurt am Main; Berlin; Brussels; Vienna; Oxford: Lang.
ISBN 0-8204-6305-1

Cover design by Lisa Barfield

275 Seventh Avenue, 28th Floor, New York, NY 10001
www.peterlangusa.com

This collection is dedicated to the contributors
for their encouragement and unflagging support.

CONTENTS

Jeffrey Andrew Weinstock

INTRODUCTION

The Pedagogical Imperative: Charlotte Perkins Gilman's "The Yellow Wall-paper"

Charlotte Perkins Gilman's short narrative, "The Yellow Wall-paper," is one of the most remarkable success stories in contemporary literary history. Although Julie Bates Dock's survey of the publication history of the story in her *Charlotte Perkins Gilman's "The Yellow Wall-paper" and the History of Its Publication and Reception: A Critical Edition and Documentary Casebook* indicates that, following its 1892 debut in *The New England Magazine*,[1] the story was republished at least twenty-three times (primarily in anthologies of supernatural tales), it was the 1973 reissue of the story by the Feminist Press accompanied by an afterword by Elaine R. Hedges that initiated a "renaissance" in Gilman studies (Dock 10). In Hedges' "Afterword," she begins by describing the tale as a "small literary masterpiece" that lamentably has been overlooked for almost fifty years (37).[2]

Although the reemergence of the story was not immediate following the Feminist Press edition, and, as late as 1985, Conrad Shumaker was able to write that "the work is highly spoken of by those who have read it, but it is not widely known and has been slow to appear in anthologies of American literature" (242), by the end of the 1980s, the incorporation of the "The Yellow Wall-paper" into the canons of American and feminist literature was complete.

Susan S. Lanser accepts the canonization of the text as a foregone conclusion when she writes in her important 1989 essay "Feminist Criticism, 'The Yellow Wallpaper,' and the Politics of Color in America," that "The canonization of 'The Yellow Wallpaper' is an obvious sign of the degree to which contemporary feminism has transformed the study of literature" (225–26). In 1992, Elaine Hedges, casting a backward glance over the development of the field of criticism on the story in her "'Out at Last'? 'The Yellow Wallpaper' after Two Decades of Feminist Criticism" is able to observe that, not only has the story become the Feminist Press's best-selling publication, but it is also "one of the best-selling works of fiction by university presses in the United States. It has been reprinted in England, France, Spain, the Netherlands, Germany, Sweden, and Iceland, and has inspired several film and dramatic versions, a television adaptation, and even an opera" (319). Furthermore, whereas Shumaker had indicated that the story was slow to be incorporated into anthologies in 1985, Hedges is able to note that "It is of course regularly assigned in women's studies and literature courses and is by now firmly established in the literary canon, appearing in all of the major anthologies" (319). These observations allow Hedges to conclude that "Together with *The Awakening* it is probably the most well-known rediscovered work by a nineteenth-century American woman" (319).

The importance of the text for feminist readers and critics cannot be overstated. Despite the controversies attendant upon the conclusion of the story and the tale's status as exemplum of female oppression, Haney-Peritz noted in 1986 that, within the canon of feminist literature, the tale had assumed "monumental proportions" (192), an observation that is echoed by William Veeder when he writes that the story is "one of the premier women's texts" (40) and by Lanser when she refers to the tale as "An American feminist classic" (225) and as a "sacred" text (226).[3] (Dock rather acidly remarks upon the canonization of Gilman when she calls into question the veracity of the "Gilman hagiography" [3, 16] that establishes Gilman as abused by male editors and that characterizes the story as a "victimized piece of literature" [2] misunderstood by the reading public in general.)

However, early in the new millennium, Charlotte Perkins Gilman's "The Yellow Wall-paper" has emerged not only as a document important to feminist scholars or even as one of the best-known and most often-taught texts by a nineteenth-century American woman, but as one of the most vital texts in English, regardless of period or sex of the author. Dock notes that "Omitting 'The Yellow Wall-paper' from an American literature anthology has become almost as unthinkable as leaving out 'The Raven' or 'Civil Disobedience'" (1).[4] Erskine and Richards are able to observe in 1993 that the story has "received more critical attention than perhaps any other American short story" (3). And, whereas Hedges had referred to the text as a "small literary masterpiece" in 1973, Ann Heilman, in a perhaps slightly hyperbolic assessment, asserts in her essay in Golden and Zangrando's *The Mixed Legacy of Charlotte Perkins Gilman* (2000) that "The Yellow Wall-paper" is today regarded as "an almost unparalleled literary masterpiece" (175).

In roughly a twenty-five-year period, the text, therefore, has gone from being considered an overlooked tale to one of the most anthologized stories in the English language. The publication history of "The Yellow Wall-paper" bears out Dock's assertion that "The story appears not just in hefty, two-volume collections of American literature, but in textbooks for women's studies and genre studies courses, and more especially in the dozens of introductory literature texts that undergraduates purchase by the gross" (1). Beyond the world of the ivory tower, the frequency of the publication of "The Yellow Wall-paper" in decidedly less-than-scholarly collections of horror stories and suspense tales such as Alberto Manguel's *Black Water 2: More Tales of the Fantastic* and Robert Phillips's *The Omnibus of 20th Century Ghost Stories*[5] suggests that the tale also holds appeal for readers with less pedantic tastes.

It is precisely the ubiquity of Gilman's story in such a diversity of settings that served as the impetus for this collection. Prior to coming across Dock's recapitulation of the publishing history of the text, I already had noted with interest the frequency with which the text was being included on college syllabi of colleagues, and what impressed me even more was the variety of thematic foci able to accommodate Gilman's narrative. I myself had included the text in a survey course on American literature, a freshman composition course, a course on feminist theory, and a course on the American ghost story. Other colleagues in English departments were using the narrative in the context of courses devoted to autobiography, American realism, and madness and literature. I learned that, outside of English departments, the text was being utilized in women's studies seminars and in a course on medicine and literature offered through a medical school. Searching on-line, I discovered the text included in courses around the world offered under the auspices of history departments, American studies programs, and psychology departments.

This diversity of academic settings able to accommodate Gilman's story impressed upon me its flexibility as a pedagogical organ. However, given the ubiquity of the text within various academic settings, I was also struck by the absence of attention to the text within pedagogical contexts. Despite the large (and steadily growing) body of criticism on the story, very little of it explicitly addresses its importance as a tool to facilitate learning or various ways in which to make use of the text in the classroom.[6] The purpose of this volume, therefore, is to introduce readers to a sampling of the multiplicitous ways in which "The Yellow Wall-paper" can be employed productively in various academic contexts. My hope is that the essays here will suggest both to those new to Gilman's text and to those already intimately familiar with the story a variety of original ways of approaching Gilman's text and making use of it as a tool for teaching.

The Pedagogical Wall-paper

Gilman's "The Yellow Wall-paper" is a story that, as Golden observes, seems to "raise more questions than it answers" (19). Golden notes that "The nature of the story, the meaning of the wallpaper, the narrator's fate, her act of crawling, and whether or not the narrator has outwitted John and 'got out at last' [. . .] emerge as some of the salient issues critics debate, often in conversation with each other" (19). Indeed, as Dale M. Bauer chronicles, the story compellingly has been interpreted in multiple ways that include:

> as Gilman's autobiographical commentary on her own depression and feelings of helplessness in her first marriage to Walter Stetson; as a critique of patriarchy and of male medical practices; as a fiction about women finding voice within the constraints of masculine language; as a reflection of the invalid women who seemed to be part of an "epidemic" of invalidism, neurasthenia, and disease in nineteenth-century, white, middle-class American culture; and as a study of one woman's attempt to free herself from social constraints. (26)

According to Hedges,

> The wallpaper, as the story's key metaphor, has been read as inscribing the medical, marital, maternal, psychological, sexual, sociocultural, political, and linguistic situation of its narrator-protagonist; as an image of the situation of the woman writer and hence a way of understanding the dilemmas of female authorship; as revealing the relations between gender and reading and gender and writing; and as a demarcation of the problems of female self-representation within both the Lacanian world of the Symbolic and the capitalist world of the United States in the late nineteenth century. Analyses of the story's formal and stylistic features have variously argued for it as a realistic story, a feminist Gothic tale, and one of the earlier modernist texts. (1992, 320)

The text has been tackled from numerous different critical perspectives including biographical, feminist, deconstructive, reader response, genre studies, discourse theory, psychoanalytic, new historicist, and cultural studies.[7]

As a text that raises so many questions and which has been approached productively from so many varied perspectives, the work seems to offer a privileged opportunity for pedagogues to engage in what Paulo Freire refers to as "problem-posing" pedagogy. In brief, in Freire's famous manifesto, *The Pedagogy of the Oppressed*, he vigorously opposes what he refers to as the "banking" concept of education. In this familiar model, the teacher-student relationship has a fundamentally "narrative" character: the authoritative teacher speaks, and the passive, empty students listen and are "filled." Traditional education is thus likened to an act of "depositing." According to Freire, the "contents" of the teacher's narration tend to become "lifeless and petrified," "detached from reality, disconnected from the totality that engendered them and gave them significance" (57). Students in the banking model of education are not asked to think, but, on the contrary, are trained *not* to question.

In contrast to the banking model, Freire proposes his "problem-posing" model in which the world is not presented as natural, static, and finished. Students are not lectured to on how the world is and asked to memorize the narrated information. Rather, "reality" (as in "The Yellow Wall-paper") is presented both as a *question* and as a *process* undergoing constant transformation. The task of the students and of the teacher is to become "critical co-investigators" (67), engaged in dialogue that seeks to "demythologize" the world. Freire insists that the process of problem-posing education can only be carried out dialogically, through communication between individuals situated as equals. The classroom for Freire thus becomes a supportive environment in which student-teachers and teacher-students *risk* confronting their ignorances and accepting the unknown as an imperative toward learning.

The essays in this volume are all concerned with the pedagogical possibilities of "The Yellow Wall-paper"—how the narrative teaches and how to teach the narrative. They present diverse approaches to the story in a variety of contexts that can be employed usefully by educators in classroom situations as varied as freshman composition, literary surveys, existentialist philosophy, and literary theory. However, taken together, I would suggest that they manifest a commitment to what Freire refers to as "problem-posing education." The essays all develop approaches to Gilman's text that seek to stimulate the critical faculties of students and to structure an engagement with the text in which the student-learner is asked to consider questions to which he or she does not already know the answers.

Leading off the volume is Debra K. Peterson's cutting-edge approach to "The Yellow Wall-paper," which provides a pedagogical blueprint for those who wish to make use of contemporary technological innovations and allow students to interact with Gilman's text in a "virtual" environment. In "A Room with a View: Charlotte Perkins Gilman's 'The Yellow Wall-paper' and the Use of MOO Spaces," Peterson explores the ways in which, through the use of computers, students actually can enter into Gilman's text, explore the space of the garden and house, and ask questions of the narrator and her husband. This immersion in the narrator's world emphasizes the literary text's narrative elements—including setting and characterization—as well as provides readers with "a participatory experience revealing the existence of multiple meanings and even contradictory interpretations of Gilman's text." Peterson's approach provides a fascinating example of a technologically mediated pedagogical methodology in which students ask questions and develop and refine their interpretations based on the information that is—or is not—elicited through their process of exploration. An additional advantage of MOO Space technology is that students are brought together in the virtual space of the constructed world. An emphasis thereby is placed on the collaborative construction of meaning as students encounter and struggle with different interpretations together.

The next three chapters all approach "The Yellow Wall-paper" from particular critical or philosophical perspectives. Gilman scholar Joanne Karpinski in "'I *will* follow that pointless pattern': A Formalist Approach to 'The Yellow Wall-paper'" provides a method of engaging students who either lack experience in textual interpretation or who are suspicious of teachers who "read in" levels of meaning that are not readily apparent to them at first glance. Karpinski's formalist approach emphasizes close reading and attention to the literary devices that Gilman employs to create her artistic effects. By focusing on formal structures and paying scrupulous attention to Gilman's language, Karpinski's approach to the text leads students to recognize that values and biases are embedded in the language of the text itself. Her method is designed to foster critical thinking in students by asking them to pay careful attention to the ways in which Gilman uses language to develop the polemical intent of the text. Through this process, students who are initially resistant to the feminist implications of Gilman's tale and who suspect that the instructor is "reading in" levels of meaning can discover the ways in which the text itself leads the reader to certain conclusions regarding the narrator and her symptomology.

In "Queering 'The Yellow Wall-paper': A Pedagogic View," Jonathan Crewe returns to his famous essay "Queering 'The Yellow Wallpaper'?: Charlotte Perkins Gilman and the Politics of Form" in order to explore the ramifications of his earlier analysis from a pedagogical perspective. In this essay, Crewe is concerned with queer pedagogy, with what it means to introduce queer theory into the classroom and how one discovers the queer reading embedded in a text. Keeping company with Karpinski's formalist reading practice, Crewe focuses on the language of the text itself in order to contend that Gilman's narrative "lends itself actively and singularly to queer-feminist reading." Beginning with the prominence of the term "queer" within Gilman's text, Crewe connects this salient semantic characteristic with "a play of desire and identification within and against any prevailing norm" manifested by the narrative as a whole. By extension, the "queerness" of Gilman's text is derived from the ways in which it refuses to "signify monolithically." Thus, as with Karpinski, Crewe's close analysis of the language of the text itself allows students to reach conclusions about the ways in which meaning is generated out of the formal features of the text itself.

In "Teaching 'The Yellow Wall-paper' and Existentialism in the Classroom," Robyn S. Shaw provides an approach to Gilman's narrative that demonstrates the text's compatibility with philosophy courses or courses investigating themes of human potential and development. Whereas Karpinski and Crewes' approaches rely strongly on close attention to Gilman's text itself, Shaw juxtaposes "The Yellow Wall-paper" with Beauvoir's *The Second Sex* and Kierkegaard's *The Sickness unto Death* in order to open up larger questions of gendered existence and self-realization. Shaw elaborates an approach to Gilman that both universalizes her narrator's predicament and simultaneously personalizes it by allowing students to explore the "existential repercussions" of their own situatedness in time and space. This process of looking at "The Yellow Wall-paper" through a philosophical lens thereby allows students to appreciate the implications of Gilman's narrative for their own lives.

The next two chapters focus on "reading dialogically," that is, on juxtaposing "The Yellow Wall-paper" with other texts in order to lead students to certain conclusions. In the same way that Shaw asks students to read "The Yellow Wall-paper" alongside works of existentialist philosophy in order to arrive at an understanding concerning the relevancy of the story to their own lives, Jim O'Loughlin in "Teaching Genre Through 'The Yellow Wall-paper'" also details a pedagogical approach to the text defined by juxtaposition of texts. However, the purpose of O'Loughlin's approach is not to allow students to derive an interpretation of the text specific to them but to prompt them to discover the ways in which their interpretations are influenced by the expectations they bring to the text, their reading histories, and the generic cues the story provides. By having his students read Gilman's text alongside of either Edgar Allan Poe's "The Fall of the House of Usher" or Gloria Steinam's *Outrageous Acts and Everyday Rebellions*, O'Loughlin leads his students to question the ways in which reading practices are shaped by social contexts and to consider how generic classification structures reader expectations. Although O'Loughlin suggests these particular companion texts for "The Yellow Wall-paper," other texts could easily be substituted. As O'Loughlin indicates, the larger point of his pedagogical method is that one can never simply read the text in front of one; rather, one's process of textual interpretation is always influenced by one's reading history and social context.

Marjean D. Purinton, in her "Reading Marital Relationships: The Wallpaper in 'A Room of One's Own'," also employs an intertextual approach to Gilman in order to analyze a thematics of turn-of-the-century women's oppression and efforts at emancipation. Purinton develops a productive dialogue using "The Yellow Wall-paper" and Virginia Woolf's *A Room of One's Own* and *Mrs. Dalloway*, Susan Glaspell's play *Trifles*, and Lillian Hellman's drama *The Children's Hour* and provides discussion questions and activity suggestions for the reader interested in exploring the pedagogical possibilities of these juxtapositions. Appropriate for a course focused on issues of gender, the conversation Purinton develops among "The Yellow Wall-paper" and a variety of other texts is designed to allow students to make connections among texts written by women at the end of the nineteenth and the first part of the twentieth century and to develop a sense of the political concerns and larger social context of these women authors.

The final chapters all focus on pedagogical approaches that privilege student responses and validate student interpretations. These essays are particularly concerned with process and dialogue. Paul Reifenheiser's reader response approach is geared to allow students to develop their critical thinking faculties by encouraging students to develop their own interpretations. According to Reifenheiser, removing students from the "interpretive bondage" of believing that texts have only one "correct" interpretation and that their own insights are not valid involves a process of demonstrating that stated authorial intentions *can* be disputed as well as affirming the validity of alternative interpretations. Accordingly, Reifenheiser develops in "Interpretive Bondage: Reader Response, Authorial Intention, and Gilman's 'The Yellow Wall-paper'" an approach to Gilman's narrative that, through journal assignments, paper assignments, and class discussion, complicates the issue of authorial intent and stresses student engagement with the text. Whereas O'Loughlin's essay emphasizes the social nature of the act of reading and the ways in which interpretation is constrained by one's reading history in order to demonstrate the power of generic conventions, Reifenheiser affirms that the differing interpretations generated by diverse social backgrounds and reading histories are not necessarily incorrect. While not dismissing the value of stated authorial intentions and published interpretations, Reifenheiser's approach to the text is designed to allow students to generate their own responses to the text and to understand that their opinions and insights are not just valid but important.

Working in concert with Reifenheiser, Janet Gebhart Auten in "Helping Students Decode the Difficult Text: 'The Yellow Wall-paper' and the Sequential Response" literally asks her students to "write their way through" "The Yellow Wall-paper." Her approach to teaching Gilman's text centers on student responses and asks students to participate in the narrator's process of discovery by observing their own reactions to the complexities of Gilman's narrative. Her sequential-response journal assignment thereby seeks to engage students in tracking their own process of sense-making and to make them more conscious of and deliberate in their effort at meaning-making. Through this process, Auten asks students to become aware of the ways in which they arrive at their varying interpretations of Gilman's text. Auten's essay is also notable because, in addition to focusing on methods of teaching Gilman to students, Auten chronicles her own process of learning how to teach Gilman effectively. She discusses both her successes and her failures and thereby literalizes Freire's notion of the classroom as a community of student-teachers and teacher-students.

Rounding out the volume is Gina Wisker's "Breakdown, Breakthrough, or Brainwash? A Dialogic Approach to 'The Yellow Wall-paper'" in which Wisker describes her experience in introducing Gilman's narrative to students who have worked as nurses or who themselves have experienced depression. These students, according to Wisker, have difficulty with interpretations of the text that privilege the conclusion as positive or empowering. This attentiveness to the ambiguity of the conclusion to Gilman's text leads Wisker to develop a "dialogic" approach to the narrative focused on depression and treatment in which students are asked to hold divergent interpretations of the text in productive tension rather than to privilege a singular interpretation. Wisker's essay is especially important because it reminds us that students can have powerful affective responses to Gilman's story—or to any story. As instructors, we need to remember that the diverse backgrounds and histories our students bring with them may allow them to identify or connect with the texts we teach in ways that, in fact, are not available to us as pedagogues. Gilman's text is one that raises disturbing issues and has the power to frustrate and unsettle. Part of teaching such a text is recognizing the power the text has to impact on the lives of its readers.

The Pedagogical Imperative

The essays in this volume all seek to develop the pedagogical possibilities of "The Yellow Wall-paper" and to provide models for others to consider, borrow from, manipulate, and appropriate. However, they are additionally connected through their attentiveness to student insights and the possibilities of "problem-posing pedagogy." What they all respond to on a certain level is what I consider to be the "pedagogical imperative" built into Gilman's now-famous text. I would like now to suggest briefly in conclusion one possible explanation for the contemporary academic reappraisal of "The Yellow Wall-paper."

From a certain perspective, what "The Yellow Wall-paper" can be said to dramatize is a failed pedagogical event. The character John within Gilman's narrative serves not only as husband, doctor, and, as critics have often observed, father, to the narrator but, as has often been implicit in critical discussions of the text, *teacher* as well; part of the infantilization of the narrator is the disabusement and dismissal of her ideas and instruction in John's way of thinking. John takes pains to teach her the "correct" way to appreciate her situation and manifests concern particularly when his wife ventures an opinion that does not coincide with his own. A priority of John's is that the narrator not think for herself but rather accept his interpretation of her symptoms and the course of treatment he prescribes.

What the reader discovers, however, is that John is a very bad teacher. His banking model of pedagogy in which he construes the narrator as an empty vessel and attempts to "fill" her with his interpretation of her condition not only devalues his pupil's intelligence and deflates her self-esteem but also engenders resentment and ultimately facilitates a psychotic break. The narrator does not learn the lesson she is supposed to learn; the disciplining of her body does not produce a concomitant subordination of mind. Rather, deprived of the opportunity to express herself and to engage in meaningful dialogue about her thoughts and feelings, the narrator develops her own discordant interpretation of her condition in secret. The revelation to John of the incongruity between his confident assertion of the narrator's fitness and the "reality" of her mental state constitutes the dramatic irony of the narrative's conclusion. "The Yellow Wall-paper" thereby stages what I consider to be a failed pedagogical encounter. John, through the arrogant foreclosure of productive dialogue and the dismissal of his wife/pupil's interpretations which lead to her mental breakdown, demonstrates the detrimental effects of a pedagogy that disregards the critical faculties of the student and treats him or her as a "container" without positive content to be filled by the teacher.

Through the dramatization of this failure of learning, Gilman thereby provides a model for both conjugal felicity and productive pedagogy. Implicit in Gilman's representation of the stifling effects of marriage on nineteenth-century white middle-class women is the two-fold message that women do indeed have their own thoughts and ideas and that, beyond simply possessing them, these thoughts and ideas need to be expressed, communicated, and validated. John, in attempting to teach his wife about herself, fails to listen to her and indeed actively dissuades her from developing her own ideas. In the end, he learns a dramatic lesson about the ignorance underlying his arrogance and its consequences. Through this representation, what Gilman provides is a dialogic model applicable not only to marriage and medicine but to the classroom as well. One may propose that had John brought his medical knowledge to bear upon the narrator's situation in such a way that took seriously her assessments of her situation and her personal desires—one that allowed her to express her interpretation of her symptoms and that validated that interpretation as significant—the dramatic breakdown at the end of the narrative might have been averted and John might have learned something about both his wife's and his own needs and desires in the process. "The Yellow Wall-paper" is thus designed to teach a lesson to the reader about the destructive effects of gender inequality and communications breakdown through the fictive representation of mental derangement and psychic crisis resulting from infelicitous pedagogical encounters. In other words, I suggest that Gilman's narrative attempts to teach a lesson by depicting for the reader failures of effective teaching and learning. Part of the appeal of "The Yellow Wall-paper" to contemporary scholars may then be that the text teaches about learning and, through negotiating the text, one can learn about effective and ineffective teaching.

Richard Shaull writes in his introduction to *The Pedagogy of the Oppressed* that "education either functions as an instrument which is used to facilitate the integration of the younger generation into the logic of the present system and bring about conformity to it, *or* it becomes 'the practice of freedom,' the means by which men and women deal critically and creatively with reality and discover how to participate in the transformation of their world" (15). If ever there was a story concerned with the necessity of transforming the world, it is "The Yellow Wall-paper." The essays in this collection are offered with the hope that, through developing various ways to introduce the story in academic settings, they may participate in this task.

A Note on the Text

As the overview of the popularity of "The Yellow Wall-paper" presented above suggests, the text is readily available in various anthologies and critical editions.[8] I have asked contributors to this volume to standardize references to the text by making use of the 1892 *New England Magazine* version in Julie Bates Dock's *Charlotte Perkins Gilman's "The Yellow Wall-paper" and the History of Its Publication and Reception: A Critical Edition and Documentary Casebook*. I am aware that Dock's commentary on the critical history of Gilman's narrative is disputed and, as Jim O'Loughlin observes, can be seen as downplaying or discrediting feminist involvement in the reemergence of the narrative. However, Dock's preparation of the text is scrupulous, and her explanation of her editorial methodology is exceptionally thorough. In keeping with the decision to make use of this edition of Gilman's text, I have asked contributors to standardize spelling of the title of the story as "The Yellow Wall-paper."

Notes

1. The publication date for the story has caused a certain amount of confusion. As Golden notes in an endnote, "The Yellow Wall-paper" first appeared in vol. 5, no. 5 (January 1892) of *The New England Magazine*, and authorship was attributed to Charlotte Perkins Stetson. Golden observes that critics have variously listed the story's original date of publication as May 1891, January 1892, and May 1892 and speculates that "The confusion surrounding the date no doubt stems from the way in which journals were bound at the time. While today we bind volumes by year, *The New England Magazine* at the turn of the century did not. Volume 5 contains six volumes, beginning with September 1891 through February 1892." Golden also notes that Gilman, in her autobiography *The Living of Charlotte Perkins Gilman*, reprints a letter that suggests the story was published in May 1891 (19, endnote 1).
2. Dock's survey of the publication history of the story refutes the critical-commonplace "legend" that the text was out of print for half a century.
3. It should be noted that both Haney-Peritz and Lanser raise the issue of the text's canonization in order to critique unqualified approval of the text's narrator (Haney-Peritz) and the status of the text as representative of female disempowerment in general (Lanser).
4. There is a certain irony in Dock's invocation of Poe and Thoreau at the beginning of her chapter entitled "The Legend of 'The Yellow Wall-paper." As Dock observes, one of the unfounded publication "legends" surrounding the text is that late nineteenth- and early twentieth-century readers failed to appreciate it as political commentary and, instead, received it "as a ghost story written in the tradition of Edgar Allan Poe" (Dock 18, citing 1993 Macmillan text *Worlds of Fiction*). According to Dock, "By dint of repetition and oversimplification, the legend [of the reception of the tale as a simple ghost story] has become firmly entrenched in Gilman studies, despite the lack of evidence to support it" (18). Her reference to Poe on the first page of her careful critique of Gilman "mythology" (16) implicitly forges an association between Poe and Gilman that Dock will later dispute.

   It is also worth noting that, in her chapter on legends and mythologies that takes certain academics to task for scholastic errors, Dock replicates a myth concerning Thoreau. As the editors of the *Heath Anthology of American Literature* observe, Thoreau's essay which is commonly referred to as "Civil Disobedience" was actually titled "Resistance to Civil Government" when it was first published in 1849 and note, "Diligent search has unearthed no evidence that the often used title, 'Civil Disobedience,' was Thoreau's" (*Heath* 2093).
5. The inclusion of Gilman's 1892 narrative in the latter testifies to a rather loose interpretation of "20th century"!
6. In Shelley Fisher Fishkin's "Reading Gilman in the Twenty-First Century," Fishkin speculates on what aspects of Gilman's writing in general will remain compelling to twenty-first century undergraduates. In "A Map for Rereading: Or, Gender and the Interpretation of Literary Texts," Annette Kolodny suggests that study of "The Yellow Wall-paper" can assist men in learning to "apprehend the meanings encoded in

texts by and about women" in the same way that "women have learned to be sensitive readers of Shakespeare and Milton, Hemingway and Mailer" (163).

7. See Hedges, 1992, p. 319.
8. Critical editions of the text include Catherine Golden's *The Captive Imagination: A Casebook on* The Yellow Wallpaper (1992); Thomas L. Erskine and Connie L. Richard's Rutgers University Women Writers: Texts and Contexts edition (1993); Dale Bauer's Bedford Cultural edition (1998); and Julie Bates Dock's *Charlotte Perkins Gilman's "The Yellow Wall-paper" and the History of Its Publication and Reception: A Critical Edition and Documentary Casebook* (1998). Other notable editions of the text include, of course, the Elaine Hedges 1973 Feminist Press version, as well as Ann Lane's *The Charlotte Perkins Gilman Reader* (1980) and Denise Knight's *"The Yellow Wall-paper" and Selected Stories of Charlotte Perkins Gilman* (1994).

Works Cited

Bauer, Dale M., Ed. *The Yellow Wallpaper*. Boston and New York: Bedford Books, 1998.

Dock, Julie Bates, Comp. and Ed. *Charlotte Perkins Gilman's "The Yellow Wall-paper" and the History of Its Publication and Reception: A Critical Edition and Documentary Casebook*. University Park, PA: The Pennsylvania State University Press, 1998.

Erskine, Thomas L., and Connie L. Richards, Eds. *"The Yellow Wallpaper."* New Brunswick, NJ: Rutgers University Press, 1993.

Fishkin, Shelley Fisher. "Reading Gilman in the Twenty-First Century." *The Mixed Legacy of Charlotte Perkins Gilman*. Eds. Catherine J. Golden and Joanna Schneider Zangrando. Newark & London: University of Delaware Press, 2000. 209–222.

Freire, Paulo. *The Pedagogy of the Oppressed*. Trans. Myra Bergman Ramos. New York: Continuum Publishing Group, 1982.

Golden, Catherine, Ed. *The Captive Imagination: A Casebook on* The Yellow Wallpaper. New York: The Feminist Press, 1992.

Golden, Catherine J., and Joanna Schneider Zangrando, Eds. *The Mixed Legacy of Charlotte Perkins Gilman*. Newark & London: University of Delaware Press, 2000.

Haney-Peritz, Janice. "Monumental Feminism and Literature's Ancestral House: Another Look at 'The Yellow Wallpaper.'" *The Captive Imagination: A Casebook* on The Yellow Wallpaper. Ed. Catherine Golden. New York: The Feminist Press, 1992. 261–276.

Heath Anthology of American Literature, V. 1. Third Edition. Ed. Paul Lauter, *et al.* Boston and New York: Houghton Mifflin Company, 1998.

Hedges, Elaine. "Afterword." *The Yellow Wallpaper*. Charlotte Perkins Gilman. Ed. Elaine Hedges. New York: The Feminist Press, 1973. 37–63.

———. "'Out at Last'? 'The Yellow Wallpaper' after Two Decades of Feminist Criticism." *The Captive Imagination: A Casebook on* The Yellow Wallpaper. Ed. Catherine Golden. New York: The Feminist Press, 1992. 319–333.

Heilman, Ann. "Overwriting Decadence: Charlotte Perkins Gilman, Oscar Wilde, and the Feminization of Art in 'The Yellow Wall-Paper'." *The Mixed Legacy of Charlotte Perkins Gilman*. Eds. Catherine J. Golden and Joanna Schneider Zangrando. Newark & London: University of Delaware Press, 2000. 175–188.

Knight, Denise D., Ed. *"The Yellow Wall-Paper" and Selected Stories of Charlotte Perkins Gilman*. Newark: University of Delaware Press, 1994.

Kolodny, Annette. "A Map for Rereading: Or, Gender and the Interpretation of Literary Texts." *The Captive Imagination: A Casebook on* The Yellow Wallpaper. Ed. Catherine Golden. New York: The Feminist Press, 1992. 149–167.

Lane, Ann J., Ed. *The Charlotte Perkins Gilman Reader: "The Yellow Wallpaper" and Other Fiction*. New York: Pantheon Books, 1980.

Lanser, Susan S. "Feminist Criticism, 'The Yellow Wallpaper,' and the Politics of Color in America." *"The Yellow Wallpaper."* Eds. Thomas L. Erskine and Connie L. Richards. New Brunswick, NJ: Rutgers University Press, 1993. 225–256.

Shaull, Richard. "Foreword." *The Pedagogy of the Oppressed*. Paulo Freire. 1970. Trans. Myra Bergman Ramos. New York: Continuum Publishing Group, 1982.

Shumaker, Conrad. "'Too Terribly Good To Be Printed': Charlotte Gilman's 'The Yellow Wallpaper." *The Captive Imagination: A Casebook on* The Yellow Wallpaper. Ed. Catherine Golden. New York: The Feminist Press, 1992. 242–252.

Veeder, William. "Who Is Jane? The Intricate Feminism of Charlotte Perkins Gilman." *Arizona Quarterly* 44.3 (Autumn 1988): 40–70.

Debra K. Peterson

A ROOM WITH A VIEW

Charlotte Perkins Gilman's "The Yellow Wall-paper" and the Use of MOO Spaces

Writing and wallpaper, woman and world. These components act as the foundation and mortar of the world of Charlotte Perkins Gilman's "The Yellow Wall-paper." A notable observation about the importance of both writing and place is found in Sandra Gilbert and Susan Gubar's discussion of the story's conclusion in *The Madwoman in the Attic*. Here, Gilbert and Gubar claim the narrator, by tearing the wallpaper, effects an "escape from her textual/architectural confinement" (147). In her opening essay to *The Captive Imagination*, Catherine Golden reinforces the importance scholars place on Gilman's complex intersections of textuality and spatiality: "[. . .] the experience of following all the criticism of 'The Yellow Wallpaper' begins to mimic that of the fictional narrator as she struggles to read the ever-changing text of the wallpaper and follow it to some sort of conclusion: the story evolves before our eyes and gains new definition" (2). Combined, Gilman's story and the criticism that surrounds it call for an approach to teaching "The Yellow Wall-paper" that recognizes the story's emphasis on text and space.[1]

As a medium for storytelling, Multi-User Domain, Object-Oriented Spaces (commonly known as MUDs/MOOs or MOO spaces) provide just such an approach. A MOO space is a virtual environment that spatializes a story. A MOO space can emphasize the literary text's use of narrative elements by re-presenting the story through the electronic creation of its buildings, rooms, furniture, and other objects. It offers innovative opportunities for analysis in its depiction of a text's world. Students exposed to a MOO space depicting Charlotte Perkins Gilman's "The Yellow Wall-paper" are immersed in a virtual world of that short story, but they also occupy and alter that world with their own virtual bodies. Confined, claustrophobic, confused, yet still curious, students find themselves in an *architextural* version of Gilman's world.[2] MOOs allow students to interact with a text, often using nothing more complicated than a Telnet connection.[3] As an essential component of this interaction, students participate in the text's (re)construction to explore its multiple meanings, meanings which are influenced by readers' cultural contexts and experiences. In these ways, MOOs create virtual worlds that hone students' analytical engagement with texts. A MOO space of "The Yellow Wall-paper," then, offers an environment where the benefits for teaching literature are twofold. First, students' interactions with and within this digital environment develop analytical skills. Second, the MOO space provides a participatory experience that reveals the existence of the multiple meanings and even contradictory interpretations of Gilman's text.[4]

The MOO Space as Interactive and Participatory

As digital environments that are both interactive and participatory, MOOs extend students' involvement with a text by offering its virtual representation. MOOs distinguish themselves from other digital technologies in their emphasis on textual constructions of both virtual worlds and social interactions. Because of these qualities, MOOs can emphasize a literary text's use of narrative elements by recreating that world: characters, setting, mood, and so forth. As has been observed by many scholars, notably Polly Wynn Allen throughout her work *Building Domestic Liberty*, Gilman was concerned with spatial dynamics and demonstrated a similar architectural richness in her writings. In "The Yellow Wall-paper," for example, Gilman details the wallpaper and the nursery as well as provides information on the rest of the "hereditary estate." When developed for the study of literature, MOOs can reinforce the importance of students' interactions with texts. The creation of virtual spaces and their objects provides a digital materiality to the imagined world of the story and to its readers. MOOs reinforce the importance of participants who visit, explore, shape, and reshape that world. In her work on MOO spaces and language, bodies, and places, Beth Kolko examines this relationship between text and reader in a digital environment: "Each movement within virtual space necessitates conceptualizing the virtual body's relation to what surrounds" (258).

Further, the use of these spaces' synchronous communication abilities—real-time online communication—is useful for discussions about literature and its interpretation. A MOO space, then, offers opportunities for analysis through its depiction of a text. Indeed, considering a MOO's characteristics offers possibilities for integrating computer technology and literature, not by substituting for literary texts but by utilizing digital environments to enhance those texts.

Integrating technology with Gilman's story necessitates recognizing and understanding the qualities of digital environments. Janet H. Murray examines the potential intersection of narratives and digital environments in her work on emerging technologies, *Hamlet on the Holodeck*. She claims digital media may be characterized broadly as having both interactive and immersive qualities. Interactivity consists of a combination of a specific digital medium's procedural and participatory designs. Though digital environments are structured procedurally, they encourage user participation and are therefore "appealing to use not just because they exhibit rule-generated behavior but because we can induce the behavior" (74). For Murray, the digital environment's participatory element is essential to its interactivity—an individual's awareness and application of a medium's "rules" is an inherent part of that environment's design and success. A digital environment's interactive nature is complemented by its immersive quality or the presentation of the medium as spatial and encyclopedic. Immersiveness helps create a space that appears to be as real as reality. In digital environments, immersion adds a transformative nature to the interactive experience. Being in a digital environment, one that (re)creates a world virtually, encourages individuals' attempts to control their experiences within that environment by negotiating that world's structures and codes. In turn, the environment becomes even more immersive as these participants contribute to the media's spatial and encyclopedic properties. In digital environments, then, immersion begets interactivity and interactivity results in immersion.

Murray's observations about the immersive and interactive properties of digital environments suggest there are obvious applications—and appeals—for teaching literature in the digital environment of MOO spaces. Because MOOs are interactive environments, both participatory and procedural, students learn the value of understanding and mastering texts in a manner that emphasizes the importance of applying tools to structures in a process similar to literary analysis. But while Murray's dual categories of interactivity and immersion are useful, this essay's discussion of MOO spaces and literature benefits from a focus on the medium's interactive and participatory characteristics, considering the manner in which the two are distinct as well as how they overlap. The interactive within the digital environment indeed is essential as within literary analysis, but it is beneficial also to reflect on the participatory experience as itself useful for enhancing students' textual interactions.

To this end, examining the possibilities for teaching literature in a MOO space necessitates offering this distinction between two terms. Simply put, interactivity involves the tools and methods students utilize when analyzing a text's constructions and meanings: textual evidence, theoretical perspectives, secondary sources, as well as those aspects specific to the digital environment. Broadly, then, interaction refers to students' intellectual activities that demonstrate a knowledge of the conventions of literary analysis. This focus on analysis as interaction develops an understanding of digital environment's rule-generated behavior and its structural procedures. Learning to engage with a text by examining the connections between its structure and its applications recalls Catherine Golden's work on the narrator and her use of language in "The Yellow Wall-paper," while it also suggests students' interactions in MOO spaces can explore the "multiplicities of meaning" that the text and its reception have generated ("One Hundred Years," 13).

Such interactivity is not, however, the only way to engage with a work, as its companion term, participatory, indicates. My interest in the benefits of a MOO space's participatory nature identifies, alternately, the process of making meaning of a text that derives from students' individual or collective experiences. This focus echoes Jean Kennard's integration of feminist and reader-response theory in her examination of Gilman's text, a move that in part utilizes Stanley Fish's "interpretive communities." As both Kennard and reader-response theorists acknowledge, readers are active creators of meanings based upon their prior experiences and expectations. Kennard introduces the notion of conventions as communities that include literary and non-literary experiences (171–74). Reader-response theory and Kennard's individual work remain useful for examining "The Yellow Wall-paper," though neither sufficiently addresses digital environments' rapidly evolving complexities, especially for how a MOO space's participatory nature involves responses to being embodied or inscribed in the world of a text.[5] Readers' experiences in MOOs are mediated constantly by the world's textuality, which, in turn, allows individuals simultaneously to analyze the text, to occupy, and even alter the architextural world, and to communicate these experiences with others. The participatory experience permits readers to exert a degree of control over the text. They may choose where to locate their virtual bodies or they may control what parts of the virtual world to explore and to what extent. They also may choose with whom to communicate during discussions. These types of participatory environments, in their focus on multiple experiences and meanings, are inherently collaborative.[6] They do not privilege either hierarchical productions—author to teacher to student—or linear productions—story to secondary sources to student work.

Both the interactive and the participatory are useful concepts for the use of MOO spaces with literature, particularly because MOO spaces are textual and social environments that rely heavily upon participants. In their introduction to *High Wired*, Cynthia Haynes and Jan Rune Holmevik use the word *cypher/TEXT* to describe the essential relationship between a MOO's textuality and its participatory nature:

> While traditional text can be thought of as one-dimensional and linear [. . .] *cypher/TEXT* adds a third dimension by bringing the reader/writer actively *into* the text. In the MOO, the reader is represented by textual descriptions. You interact with others through textual dimensions, through textual ethos, pathos, and logos. Thus, readers speak, emote, and think in several dimensions, but more than that—they *are* a textual dimension in and of themselves. (11)

Haynes and Holmevik's work emphasizes how these spaces and their participants are interrelated, with participants having as much of an effect on the space as the space has on its participants. MOOs are clearly useful for Gilman's text, especially as Gilman claimed to be less interested in literature for its aesthetic qualities than its didactic and transformative possibilities. As she said about her interest in writing, "it is a pretty poor thing to write, to talk, without a purpose" (*Living*, 121).

A Room with a View: "The Yellow Wall-paper" Estate MOO Space

Gilman's "The Yellow Wall-paper" offers a rich site for exploring various interpretations of the text, whether informed by biographical, new historicist, reader-response, cultural studies or feminist theorizations, or through different pedagogical strategies. Whether beginning student or budding scholar, students collectively tend to view the nursery, with its double presence of the narrator and the wallpaper, as a mystery to be solved. Their reactions have some provocative insights as to the attraction of literature more generally, ones better discussed at length in another essay. Still, it is worth noting that part of the joy of reading mysteries stems from the opportunity to work with textual evidence and to struggle with different interpretive possibilities. As a substantial part of students' interest in Gilman's story derives from how it lends itself to interpretation, my design and use of a MOO space based upon "The Yellow Wall-paper" attempt to evoke a similar engagement.

Once connected to the educational MOO that hosts the MOO space of "The Yellow Wall-paper," students encounter Gilman's text through the virtual extensions of their physical bodies. This experience is substantially different than rereading the text. Students enter simple programming commands that control their textual bodies and behaviors as they "move" inside the space. Also in this way, they may "look" at their surroundings, touch or otherwise manipulate objects, and engage in conversation with each other or programmed robots, all of which is accomplished by reading descriptions and writing responses.[7] By typing commands, students may execute a series of directions to navigate their bodies from the general entrance of a MOO space to the specific site designated by the instructor.[8]

An interest in students' participation and interaction informed my decision to use "The Yellow Wall-paper" as the foundation and frame for my MOO space and, when possible, to present architextural descriptions. The space attempts to invoke the tone of Gilman's work in much the same way filmmakers and playwrights transform a literary story for another medium. Its design is concerned with how students experiencing "The Yellow Wall-paper" Estate, as it has been entitled, might react to an explicitly spatial re-presentation. As a result, the Estate resembles Gilman's story translated into a virtual pathway, garden, house, and nursery with robots programmed to represent the narrator and John.[9] Recreating the narrator's world in this way recognizes Gilman's interest in architecture and in how domestic spaces require both the analysis and transformation of their material and ideological constructions (Gaudelius 118–19; Allen).

These interests led to a design that attempts to provide students with a spatial experience for exploration of Gilman's text without architexturally leading them to privilege any one analysis. The space itself contains no secondary sources. Although it is possible to construct a pedagogically sound space on "The Yellow Wall-paper" that incorporates the primary text, historical context, and critical analyses as part of its structure, this example focuses on Gilman's 1892 text. Remembering Annette Kolodny's comments about the narrator's experience, students here have the opportunity to "discover a consistent and coherent pattern amid the 'sprawling outlines' of the wallpaper's apparently 'pointless pattern'" (156). It should be noted, however, that while MOO spaces lend themselves easily to depictions of spatial structures such as gardens and rooms, the recreation of literal spaces for "The Yellow Wall-paper" is but one design possibility. It is equally viable to design a MOO space as a diary in keeping with the text's diary-entry structure. An alternate design might resemble a theater set, with students assuming the roles of John or the narrator; this option might be useful for students in a role-playing activity or for a class focusing on questions of identity. All design options, of course, do represent an analysis of their own, and students are encouraged to interrogate the design—and its inclusions and exclusions—as such.

Because the purpose of the Estate MOO space is to act as a supplement to the short story, there are some necessary alterations to Gilman's text. To facilitate students' exploration of the space, it is an active revisiting of the story. Students may question the robot of Jane, as the narrator is called within the MOO space in order to keep her distinct from classroom discussions of the narrator.[10] They then receive programmed responses cued by the key words of their questions. Or they may decide to focus entirely on the wallpaper, even attempt to tear it down. Students may choose to interrogate John, another robot, or refuse to listen to him at all. They may search the nursery for Jane's secret writing. Students may multitask while they participate in an online classroom discussion about Gilman's text. Regardless of their decisions, students collectively affect the space because their bodies' behaviors textually register on all participants' screens, potentially recorded and saved for later analysis.

In the following exchanges, excerpts from a visit to "The Yellow Wall-paper" Estate demonstrate how this MOO space textually represents Gilman's story and suggest how students may interact with both versions of "The Yellow Wall-paper."

```
@exits

Obvious exits: south, north, hut, and estate.

estate

The Yellow Wallpaper Estate

The most beautiful place! It is quite alone, standing well
back from the road, quite three miles from the village. It
makes you think of English places that you have read about.
There are hedges and walls and gates that lock and many sep-
arate little houses for the gardeners and people. To the
north is a *knot_garden* that leads up to a colonial man-
sion. You may also take the long dirt *road* out to leave
"The Yellow Wallpaper" Estate. (30)
```
[11]

There are minor changes to Gilman's text that are largely navigational. They contribute to Gilman's text by suggesting what parts of the space students might explore. Most other changes are those that permit participants to experience "The Yellow Wall-paper" Estate as virtual bodies which occupy the same space as the narrator. The changes allow students to see Gilman's virtual world through the narrator's descriptions, the bot Jane's words, and their own actions. To make the MOO experience more effective, these changes in Gilman's text are substantial. As mentioned above, the narrator is represented by a programmed robot called Jane, an alteration that is not unproblematic.[12] There is also a shift in the story's first-person narration to second person in an attempt to place students more fully in "The Yellow Wall-paper." This shift is evident immediately upon entering.

```
The Colonial Mansion
It is very seldom that mere ordinary people like John and
Jane can secure ancestral halls for the summer. A colonial
mansion, a hereditary estate, one would say a haunted house
and reach the height of romantic felicity—but that would be
asking too much of fate! You have heard something about some
legal trouble, something about the heirs and co-heirs; any-
how, the place has been empty for years. But there is some-
thing strange about the house—you can feel it. The feeling
is not so much in the garden to the north and through the
*gate*, where John sits on a bench. No, the strangeness
comes from inside the nursery, which is just up the *stairs*.
To the south are the *hedges* and gardens that border the es-
tate. (29-30)
```

Of course, these alterations are significant ones that should be addressed in class discussions, but the discussion itself can prove fruitful for interacting with the text. For instance, the change that occurs with the shift to second person can lead to a consideration of how the first-person point of view is essential to analyzing the text in terms of language and structure.[13]

To emphasize a participatory moment and encourage student interaction, however, the shifts are necessary, particularly the shift in perspective. Shifting the point of view to second person enhances the architextural world's interactive properties. With students surrounded by and implicated in the text, the MOO becomes a different, complementary experience to reading Gilman's story. The MOO space becomes, as Haynes and Holmevik suggest with *cypher/TEXT*, the students' world to discover, to challenge, and to change. The point of view creates the illusion that readers "see" the narrator's world through her descriptions—as the bot Jane sees it, yet not *through* her eyes but through their own. Their reactions to the yellow wallpaper are transformed because it is not Jane alone who experiences this place, it is also the students via their bodies who become the "you" in the descriptions. By offering a degree to which students may experience the nursery, the point of view reinforces the setting's effect and significance.

An obvious benefit to using a MOO as a means to examine Gilman's short story is its ability to render setting and description as the story's focus. The MOO's spatial intricacies "involve a rich combination of description and narrative, interesting ambient details, and special objects that players may activate or look at while exploring a room" (Haynes "Help!," 171). This focus is appropriate because it complements Gilman's work in spatiality, as most overtly presented in this story as well as her books *Women and Economics* and *The Home*. Although students who first attempt to navigate the labyrinthian spaces to reach the nursery often become disoriented, this initial disorientation is beneficial for experiencing Gilman's text. Students increasingly become removed from their everyday reality and dislocated when they attempt to find the nursery buried within the larger Estate. To enter the Estate, students first must stray from the "path" designed as a navigational tool for the larger MOO. Once leaving this path, students encounter a knot garden complemented by warnings, evoking fairy-tale admonitions, either to return to the path or to continue on their journey into Gilman's world. Students who go to the Estate are separated from the larger social reality of the educational MOO space in a manner similar to the narrator's separation from her world. Once there, their objective is to explore the nursery for the purpose of analysis and discussion, but they cannot do so until they learn to negotiate the different areas of the Estate and the rules of this MOO space. Like the narrator, these students are not "cured" of their situation simply by arriving at the Estate.

The MOO space's design encourages students first to examine the garden.

The Garden

A delicious garden! It is large and shady, full of box-bordered paths, and lined with long grape-covered arbors with seats under them. There are greenhouses, too, but they are all broken now. There are *trees* with shadows creeping around them. *John* is seated there, waiting for you to ask him questions. If you would rather go to the nursery, go south through the swinging gate and back to the mansion. A small gate that locks from the outside–to keep things in rather than out? (30)[14]

The lack of detail in the garden provides a tutorial for visiting the Estate's nursery and simultaneously reinforces the story's focus on the nursery, in part because the garden lacks the nursery's textual richness. Yet within the garden there are several options as to how to approach the story: look at the space, examine the objects within the space, search for the key that Jane has thrown out the window, or talk with the programmed bot of John.

Inevitably, most students choose to activate John first.

look John

Jane's husband, physician, and caretaker. You may talk with him if you type <activate John>.

activate John

John [to D. K. Peterson] : I am Jane's husband and a physician of high standing. She considers me practical, perhaps even in the extreme. But I simply have no patience with faith. I

> dislike superstitious nonsense. As a doctor, I see no purpose in any talk of things not to be felt and seen and put down in figures. (29)

Because John is a character in the story, his responses risk being authoritative, as do the responses of Jane as the narrator. Students tend to ask questions that would have John interpret the story or to react as if John were a real person. Some students ask John about his motivations, while others verbally attack John for what they perceive as his domestic abuse. Their initial treatment of a programmed bot reveals the participatory pull of the story and its MOO space, as well as its immersiveness; this space is a virtual *reality*. But John is programmed to respond only with phrases or qualities that the narrator and instructor attribute to him.

> You say, "Is Jane crazy?"
>
> John [to D. K. Peterson] : There is nothing the matter with Jane but a temporary nervous depression—a slight hysterical tendency. We rented this house, I forbid her to write, and I ordered her to rest in the nursery. But she immediately disliked the wallpaper. (25)

Other questions, particularly ones that ask for further explanations, are readdressed to the students, or they suggest that students should visit the nursery.

> You say, "What is the meaning of the wallpaper?"
>
> John [to D. K. Peterson] : I don't know. What do you think it all means?

Even those students hoping the space will provide answers to what the story "really means" quickly abandon any interrogation of John. Instead, they begin to look to the garden itself and to talk with each other. The garden, as an introduction to the space's design, encourages students to use their own observations and discussions, to ask questions of the text, and to seek their own answers rather than to seek or accept statements from an authority figure.

This initial exploration prepares students for the more detailed nursery.

> The Nursery
>
> It is a big, airy room, the whole floor nearly, with *windows* that look all ways, and air and sunshine galore. It appears to have been a nursery first and then a playroom and gymnasium. Yet all the *windows* are barred for little children, and there are rings and things in the walls. The paint and *paper* look as if a boys' school had used it. It is stripped off—the

```
paper—in great patches all around the head of the *bed*,
about as far as one can reach, and in a great place on the
other side of the room low down. You never saw a worse *wall-
paper* in your life. If you decide you would rather not visit
this odd nursery, move *downstairs*. You enter the nursery
on tiptoes. (30-31)
```

These descriptions enable looking at the room and being in the room, participating and analyzing.

```
look windows

Out of one *window* of the nursery one can see the garden,
those mysterious deep-shaded arbors, the riotous old-
fashioned flowers, and bushes and gnarly trees. . . . To jump
out of the window would be admirable exercise, but the bars
on it are too strong even to try. You are surrounded by an
unusual *wallpaper*. If you wish, you can walk down the
stairs to the garden to talk to John. (32, 41)
```

Students may look out the window, tear the wallpaper, or gnaw the bed. They, in effect, participate in the story by adopting the narrator's actions or possible actions. Students have similar restrictions and perceptions as the narrator, but they retain their autonomy and individuality. They see the wallpaper and objects as described in Gilman's text but read a condensed, even possibly more organized, narrative in the descriptions assigned to objects.[15] They may pick up and examine objects such as the bed or the journal, but they cannot remove any objects from the room.

```
look bed

This great heavy bed which looks as if it had been through
the wars. . . . It is a great immovable bed. You try to push
it against the *wall*, but it appears to be nailed
down. . . . The bedstead is fairly gnawed. It looks like
someone bit off a little piece at one corner. There appears
to be a *journal* folded up and hidden between corners of the
frame. (33-4, 41)
```

Students may choose to leave, and it is their decision to do so that contrasts with the narrator's voluntary restriction to the nursery.[16]

Complicating the too-easy distinction between students' freedom and the narrator's imprisonment, though, is the class discussion that occurs within the MOO space. To participate in class discussion students need to remain in the nursery space. Only participants who are in the room where the discussion takes place can see the textual conversation that scrolls on the computer screens; the conversations inhabit the same space as the wallpaper, Jane, and the students themselves. Moving to another space, even the garden, closes one's virtual ears and eyes.[17] But even though the compulsion to stay in the room is removed somewhat—students may leave a virtual space without creating the same type of disruption as leaving a physical classroom—students remain in order to engage with the space or to see, hear, and experience what their peers have discovered about the story. This voluntary confinement within the nursery mirrors the choice of the narrator. Heather Kirk Thomas notes that although it is the narrator who controls the key access to the nursery, her lack of physical imprisonment often surprises first-time readers (202). Students' movements, or lack of movements, in the MOO space address their presumptions about the narrator's imprisonment and the role of John as antagonist. Their reactions demonstrate the story's "psychological realism" (Schöpp-Schilling 141), while the description and constraints of the nursery help students to analyze the situation of the narrator better.

However, students' awareness of such complexities are not necessarily reflected in their interrogation of the robot of Jane, whose program is intended to integrate students' participatory behavior and analytical skills. Initially, Jane is hidden from the students, who have to examine the room closely in order to find her and the many references to the wallpaper.

```
look Jane

Here, trapped in the nursery of The Yellow Wallpaper Estate,
is Jane. She represents the first-person protagonist of Char-
lotte Perkins Gilman's short story "The Yellow Wall-paper."
Visitors experience this world through her eyes. If you would
like to talk with her, type <activate Jane>. When you have
finished your conversation, type <hush Jane>. You may also
wish to visit John in the garden.
```

Jane has a wider range of responses than John, and students address a greater number of questions to her, often of a more personal nature. Like John, Jane refuses to answer interpretive questions, especially about her (in)sanity. Instead, she repeats Gilman's text or asks what the students think. With many of these questions, Jane suggests that students should analyze their surroundings by moving to the garden, looking out the window, or examining the yellow wallpaper. All actions in a room are broadcast for everyone in the room to see, so Jane's responses are visible on everyone's computer screen. In effect, a bot's response to an individual's question benefits everyone, while any one student's conversation with Jane introduces possible directions for classroom discussion. Further, because Jane's responses encourage students to examine various objects, the importance of a literary skill—close textual analysis—is reinforced.

```
You say, "Do you love your husband?"

Jane [ to D. K. Peterson] : John laughs at me, of course, but
one expects that in marriage. . . . The fact is I am getting
a little afraid of John. . . . And John is so queer now, that
I don't want to irritate him. I wish he would take another
room! Even Jennie has an inexplicable look. I don't want
anybody to get that woman out at night but myself. I'm sure
if you talked to John in the garden he would tell a differ-
ent story. Or look for my *journal.* (29, 37, 40)
```

These questions, as well as Jane's answers, sharpen students' interpretive powers. The design offers a balance between the narrator's assertions, the story's space, and readers' analyses.

A pivotal response to these questions is Jane's suggestion to look for the narrator's journal. These writings, like those in the story, are concealed in the room. Readers must first ask Jane about the writings or closely examine the room themselves. The narrator's diary remains hidden to reposition students as active seekers and makers of meaning; in looking for the diary they are neither Jane, who knows where the writing is hidden, nor John, who does not know about the writing. Students instead adopt the roles of literary detectives. Here the students are given the opportunity to obtain that knowledge through the diaries which reveal the narrator's state of mind (Knight 9). Keeping Jane's observations about the room and the wallpaper separate from what the narrator thinks or feels helps students distinguish between the two different types of evidence. More complete knowledge about the narrator, the story, and the space becomes available to students who investigate both the room's contents and the diary.

But it is the central figure or symbol of the wallpaper that vividly combines Gilman's interest in space and writing. Judith Fetterley argues that the wallpaper functions as an expressive text with which both the narrator and the reader must struggle to understand and, ultimately, escape (259–60). With such high stakes, it is no surprise that students' attention focuses primarily on the wallpaper as they experience the space.[18] There are nine different objects constructed for this MOO space, developed from the overwhelming and even claustrophobic presence of the yellow wallpaper (Berman 232). Here, Gilman's fragmented focus permits the creation of different MOO objects to represent the wallpaper. They collectively draw attention to the wallpaper's many layers, with some objects dedicated to its color, its odor, and various other characteristics.

```
look pattern

It is dull enough to confuse the *eyes* in following, pro-
nounced enough to constantly irritate and provoke study, and
```

```
when you follow the lame uncertain curves for a little dis-
tance they suddenly commit suicide—plunge off at outrageous
angles, destroy themselves in unheard of contradictions.
. . . You think you have mastered it, but just as you get
well underway in following, it turns a back-somersault and
there you are. It slaps you in the face, knocks you down, and
tramples upon you. It is like a bad dream. . . . The wall-
paper is torn off in *spots*, and it sticketh closer than a
brother—they must have had perseverance as well as hatred.
(31, 37, 33)

look eyes

Behind that *outside* pattern the dim shapes get clearer
every day. . . . But in the places where it isn't faded and
where the *daylight* is just so—you can see a strange, pro-
voking, formless sort of figure, that seems to skulk about
behind that silly and conspicuous front design. . . . It is
always the same shape, only very numerous. And it is like a
woman stooping down and creeping about behind that pattern.
. . . You didn't realize for a long time what the thing was
that showed behind, that dim sub-pattern, but now you are
quite sure it is a woman. By daylight she is subdued, quiet.
You fancy it is the pattern that keeps her so still. It is so
puzzling. . . . You don't like it a bit. Neither does Jane—
just ask her. (35, 33, 35, 33, 37)

look daylight

There is one end of the room where it is almost intact, and
there, when the crosslights fade and the low sun shines di-
rectly upon it, you can almost fancy radiation after all—the
interminable grotesques seem to form around a common cen-
tre and rush off in headlong plunges of equal distraction.
. . . On a *pattern* like this, by daylight, there is a
lack of sequence, a defiance of law, that is a constant ir-
ritant to a normal mind. . . . In the nursery, the *moon*
shines in all around just as the sun does. (34, 37, 35)
```

Gilman's layered description of the wallpaper opens the text to multiple interpretations, a point further demonstrated by students' discussions, experiences in MOO, and application of architextural analysis.

MOOving Beyond the Text: Student Interactions

While the space's design permits examination of Gilman's text, it is the students' ability to participate that encourages them to interact with it. Although, as I note at the beginning of this essay, participation in the MOO space is useful in itself, interaction is built upon participation. Students' spatial dislocation, followed by attention to descriptive details, combines with their identification with the narrator's experience; these experiences all heighten students' investment in the story's development. Just as Gilman's story "was created for a public audience and thus invites the reader to interact with the text" (Knight 13), students' participatory experiences in the MOO space lead to interactivity.

After initial explorations of the MOO, students may engage in a synchronous discussion of "The Yellow Wall-paper" and use the space to support assertions and explore ideas. The space offers a viable alternative to traditional discussions though a MOO discussion reads/sounds considerably different from those in the traditional classroom.[19] Discussions in MOO spaces are a hybrid between orality and writing that are a result, in part, of real time discussions being typed quickly; like email or chat rooms, these conversations tend to adopt a conversational tone. Discussions in the MOO can follow multiple conversations known as threads, which scroll constantly on the screen; these discussions may be recorded, saved, and later analyzed by the instructor or the class. Their synchronous and overlapping qualities can be distracting for participants, especially if there are multiple discussions happening. But because all the discussion also textually occupies the room, a sense of collaborative community emerges which is distinct from the solitary experience of reading the text. It is a community of investigation. Students' communal MOO experiences expose different ways to approach a text and students' diverse experiences with that text. In a MOO space, students may participate in multiple discussions and adopt different standpoints or argue conflicting perspectives. It is not uncommon for one MOO session to have a discussion about the illness/madness of the narrator juxtaposed with a debate about John's patriarchal authority, which is then interrupted by another student's interrogation of Jane—in which he or she expresses frustration at the bot's repeated refusal to illuminate the whys of the text with "I don't know. What do *you* think?" The differences are present simultaneously; conversations overlap, and conflicting interpretations are examined through references to Gilman's text available in the MOO space.

Of course, like traditional classroom discussions, there can be drawbacks to virtual discussions. They tend to be less focused because students and teachers engage in less hierarchical lines of investigation. While multiple threads of conversations tease out numerous interpretations and questions, some areas do not receive the in-depth treatment others do; unlike their behaviors in more controlled environments, students really do take ownership of the class and discussion.[20] Discussions online also tend to privilege those comfortable with computer technology, much the way other discussion formats privilege those who are comfortable with those formats' codes. Once introduced and given the exposure to the skills needed to participate in MOO, however, online discussions offer every student the opportunity to participate simultaneously. In my observations, MOOs enable active and varied participation, especially from students who are silent in the traditional classroom. Perhaps because in the MOO students can more freely pursue their own areas of critical inquiry or refer easily to Gilman's text, students tend to interact more rigorously with the text or pursue their own analyses with more determination.

MOOs also permit vigorous debates between discussants without disruption of the class. Particularly vocal students have been known to have "sideline" conversations, even online shouting matches, related to their interests as the majority of the class pursues the dominant points of discussion. Overall, though, students gravitate to, as do scholars themselves, the ending's meaning. The ambiguity of the conclusion is useful to recall: "the ending of the story defies a reductive ending, no doubt as Gilman intended" (Golden, "One Hundred Years," 15). The MOO space deliberately encourages debate about the ending. Students looking for Jennie in hopes of receiving an explanation about the narrator's use of the name "Jane"—did the narrator mean in spite of *Jennie*?—at the story's end are disappointed. Jennie is not present in the space, and the bot of Jane will not address whether she meant Jennie or Jane. This leaves students to struggle with the meaning of the ending. In order to determine the conclusion's meaning, students cannot solely rely on the MOO space, Gilman's text, or the editorial footnotes that accompany different editions. They must interact with the text and assert their own conclusions, often dealing with not just the narrator's words but her actions within the space.

```
You say, "Why do you creep?"

Jane [ to D.K. Peterson] : "I am here, and no person touches
this paper but me—not alive! I finally peeled off the paper.
I had to lock the door and throw away the key so that I had
the time to free her, don't you see? And I needed the rope so
that I am securely fastened now—you don't get me out in the
road or the garden! Finally, when John came back I told him
that the key is down by the front steps, under a plantain
leaf! And he found it. . . But it was too late—I'd got out at
last in spite of John and Jane. And I'd pulled off most of
the paper, so they can't put me back! But I still don't
understand why should that man have fainted? But he did, and
right across my path by the wall, so that I had to creep over
him every time!" (41-2)
```

Still others become personally invested in discussing the text's treatment of domestic abuse and mental illness, combining their experiences in the MOO space with their analysis of the text and with their personal experiences. In this way, Gilman's story moves to contexts outside the literature classroom, suggesting that the analysis of a text is not simply a matter of "what the text means" or an individual's interpretation. Analysis includes a collaborative conversation that incorporates the text, context, scholars and teachers, and even those participants that many students had not considered previously in the construction of meaning . . . themselves.

MOO spaces' collaborative nature also offers possibilities for Gilman's text to be enhanced with writing projects based on the students' experiences. Such projects could be as simple as working with transcriptions of the group discussions and writing individual papers using this material.[21] Students could write collaboratively in MOO. They could contribute to an instructor's designed space by creating their own objects—perhaps not only those objects found in the text but also those that inform the space in other ways—illuminating the story's meaning through their analysis. The objects might be based on Gilman's autobiographical writings, for instance, or the historical context or scholarly criticism. Or students might benefit from creating a MOO space of "The Yellow Wall-paper" that offers their insights.

Common throughout these experiences is the emphasis on the collaborative construction of meaning for "The Yellow Wall-paper." Students encounter and struggle with different interpretations without working in isolation. Embedded in these activities is the use of a MOO's participatory and interactive qualities to encourage students' literary engagement and use of (architextural) evidence. With students' words literally occupying the same electronic space as Gilman's text, MOO spaces privilege both the text and its interpretation. In MOOs, students demonstrate writing and analytical skills that derive not only from their reading of a text but by their participation in it. Since their movement through Gilman's virtual world can be anticipated but not scripted, students remain actively invested and in control of their interpretations. Immersing themselves in a MOO space of "The Yellow Wall-paper," students not only interact with Gilman's text but participate in its claustrophobic space, its madness, and its meaning.

Notes

1. Catherine Golden's book *The Captive Imagination* provides a good overview on scholarship of "The Yellow Wall-paper," particularly for feminist studies. For those interested in Gilman's own interest in space, Polly Wynn Allen's *Building Domestic Liberty* is useful.
2. See Haynes and Holmevik, "Introduction: 'From the Faraway Nearby'," 4. As Sherry Turkle succinctly states in her foreword, "architextural" describes MOO writing as "a landscape of words" (x).

3. See notes 4, 8, and 9 for more information.
4. I have avoided including the technical information needed to build and use MOOs. More information may be found in Cynthia Haynes and Jan Rune Holmevik's *High Wired*.
5. My use of participatory environment is not oppositional to reader-response theory but instead focuses on the immersive digital environment that places the reader inside the text in a manner distinct from the ways in which reader-response theory addresses readers' creations of meaning.
6. Not all digital environments are equally collaborative. This is particularly true of digital environments featuring asynchronous forms of communication.
7. This is only an introduction to what may be done in MOOs. Students may also build their own MOO spaces, conduct group presentations, or engage in collaborative writing and peer editing.
8. There are several educational MOO spaces available, and many universities have begun to host their own. In order to connect to a MOO space, students need only an Internet connection and a simple program such as Telnet. There are, however, many free software programs available that make negotiating MOO spaces even easier. There also is an increasing number of web-based MOO spaces, some of which permit the incorporation of visual materials as well as text. These offer intriguing possibilities for those projects that would benefit from a visual component.
9. The MOO space entitled The Yellow Wallpaper Estate, used without the quotation marks or hyphen, was created in the Connections MOO. Connections MOO is accessible through a Telnet connection at <connections.moo.mud.org 3333>. Although I am basing my discussion upon this MOO space, there are many different types of MOO spaces and exercises that can be developed for different purposes and pedagogies.
10. To create a robot of the narrator that could talk with students without causing problems for the synchronous discussion that takes place in the same MOO room in which the robot exists, it became necessary for me to provide the robot of the narrator with a name. Otherwise, every time class discussion would address questions to the narrator by using the word "narrator," the robot would interrupt student discussion. I determined it would be less confusing to call the robot "Jane" so that students could continue to use the term narrator, thus indirectly pointing to the possible discrepancy in the two interpretations. The programming limitations, it should be noted, derive as much from the author of this paper as from the MOO space itself.
11. For clarity, I have decided to distinguish between the essay's text and the architextural space of the Yellow Wallpaper Estate by following the conventions set forth in Haynes and Holmevik's *High Wired*. The MOO space text appears in Courier font, much the way it appears on screen when inside a MOO space. The edition of "The Yellow Wallpaper" I use for MOO space citation is the 1892 edition found in Julie Bates Dock's *Charlotte Perkins Gilman's "The Yellow Wall-paper" and the History of Its Publication and Reception*. With the exception of page references to Gilman's text and minor issues of clarity or programming needs, I have left the text unaltered. For readers of this essay, I have included brief commands that participants in the MOO space would use to negotiate movement. I also have changed my MOO character name back to my RL (real-life) name. For programming reasons, the punctuation of Gilman's text was slightly altered, including the combination of different paragraphs of text and the elimination of the hyphen in "Wall-paper" in the title. When using multiple sections of Gilman's text

in the creation of a description for a single space or object, I have included the separate page numbers in order of their use.

12. See note 10.
13. For examples of this type of scholarship, please refer to Catherine Golden's "The Writing of 'The Yellow Wallpaper': A Double Palimpsest" or Paula Treichler's "Escaping the Sentence: Diagnosis and Discourse in 'The Yellow Wallpaper'," both available in *The Captive Imagination*.
14. In a MOO space, words set apart by asterisks usually indicate that the word is also an object with a separate description or function.
15. The description of an object sometimes contains several descriptions from the story. Due to programming restrictions, some of Gilman's punctuation was changed. These changes and their effects are addressed in classroom discussion. The discussions serve to emphasize the significance of structure and language in Gilman's story.
16. Jane, the bot, cannot leave the nursery space. She is programmed to remain in that space.
17. In other words, occupants in a MOO space are restricted to observing what goes on in the space where their virtual body is located. One cannot eavesdrop or participate in conversations in other "rooms" of a MOO.
18. Again, students engaging in a MOO space do not necessarily follow a linear order of exploration despite the construction of this essay, which moves from one component of the MOO space to another for clarity.
19. I acknowledge Ken Schweller's point that "there remains a significant amount of asynchronicity in the process" (89). However, MOO discussions do offer a more synchronous communication than other forms of digital communication and, I have observed, are no less synchronous than many real-time discussions in the traditional classroom.
20. I often supplement MOO discussion with a traditional class discussion that uses the electronic transcripts of the online discussion as a starting point. By returning to the recorded MOO discussion, points can be reinforced; unanswered questions may be addressed, and the strengths in students' literary analyses reinforced. Also, transcripts may be distributed to the class or posted online as future references for students to use in subsequent discussions, for writing papers, and so on. The ability to record discussions extends the initial conversation of the MOO by permitting students and teachers to return to and reflect upon class interactions.
21. The above endnote offers some possibilities for using classroom discussion in writing projects. Additionally, MOO transcripts encourage students to view each other as a community of scholars whose contributions are worthy of further investigation and may be integrated with other critical analyses.

Works Cited

Allen, Polly Wynn. *Building Domestic Liberty: Charlotte Perkins Gilman's Architectural Feminism*. Amherst: The University of Massachusetts Press, 1988.

Berman, Jeffrey. "The Unrestful Cure: Charlotte Perkins Gilman and 'The Yellow Wallpaper'." *The Captive Imagination: A Casebook on* The Yellow Wallpaper. Ed. Catherine Golden. New York: The Feminist Press, 1992. 211–41.

Dock, Julie Bates, Comp. and Ed. *Charlotte Perkins Gilman's "The Yellow Wall-paper" and the History of Its Publication and Reception: A Critical Edition and Documentary Casebook*. University Park, PA: The Pennsylvania State University Press, 1998.

Fetterley, Judith. From "Reading about Reading: 'A Jury of Her Peers,' 'The Murders in the Rue Morgue,' and 'The Yellow Wallpaper.'" *The Captive Imagination: A Casebook on* The Yellow Wallpaper. Ed. Catherine Golden. New York: The Feminist Press, 1992. 253-60.

Gaudelius, Yvonne. "Kitchenless Houses and Homes: Charlotte Perkins Gilman and the Reform of Architectural Space." *Charlotte Perkins Gilman: Optimist Reformer*. Eds. Jill Rudd and Val Gough, Iowa City: University of Iowa Press, 1999. 111–126.

Gilbert, Sandra, and Susan Gubar. From *The Madwoman in the Attic: The Woman Writer and the Nineteenth -Century Literary Imagination. The Captive Imagination: A Casebook on* The Yellow Wallpaper. Ed. Catherine Golden. New York: The Feminist Press, 1992. 145–48.

Gilman, Charlotte Perkins. *The Home: Its Work and Influence*. New York: McClure, Phillips & Company, 1903.

——. *The Living of Charlotte Perkins Gilman: An Autobiography*. New York: D. Appleton-Century Company, 1935.

——. "The Yellow Wallpaper." 1892. *Charlotte Perkins Gilman's "The Yellow Wallpaper" and the History of Its Publication and Reception: A Critical Edition and Documentary Casebook*. Comp. and Ed. Julie Bates Dock. University Park, PA: The Pennsylvania State University Press, 1998. 29–42.

——. *Women and Economics: A Study of the Economic Relation Between Men and Women as a Factor in Social Evolution*. Boston: Small, Maynard & Co, 1898.

Golden, Catherine. "One Hundred Years of Reading 'The Yellow Wallpaper.'" *The Captive Imagination: A Casebook on* The Yellow Wallpaper. Ed. Catherine Golden. New York: The Feminist Press, 1992. 1–23.

——. "The Writing of 'The Yellow Wallpaper': A Double Palimpsest." *The Captive Imagination: A Casebook on* The Yellow Wallpaper. Ed. Catherine Golden. New York: The Feminist Press, 1992. 296–306.

Haynes, Cynthia. "Help! There's a MOO in This Class." *High Wired: On the Design, Use, and Theory of Educational MOOs*. Eds. Cynthia Haynes and Jan Rune Holmevik. 1998. Ann Arbor, MI: University of Michigan Press, 2001. 161–76.

Haynes, Cynthia, and Jan Rune Holmevik. "Introduction: 'From the Faraway Nearby'." *High Wired: On the Design, Use, and Theory of Educational MOOs*. Eds. Cynthia Haynes, and Jan Rune Holmevik. 2001. Ann Arbor, MI: University of Michigan Press, 1998.

Hedges, Elaine R. "Afterword to 'The Yellow Wallpaper,' Feminist Press Edition." *The Captive Imagination: A Casebook on* The Yellow Wallpaper. Ed. Catherine Golden. New York: The Feminist Press, 1992. 123–37.

Kennard, Jean E. "Convention Coverage, or How to Read Your Own Life." *The Captive Imagination: A Casebook on* The Yellow Wallpaper. Ed. Catherine Golden. New York: The Feminist Press, 1992. 168–90.

Knight, Denise D. *Charlotte Perkins Gilman: A Study of the Short Fiction*. New York: Twayne Publishers, 1997.

Kolko, Beth. "Bodies in Place: Real Politics, Real Pedagogy, and Virtual Spaces." *High*

Wired: On the Design, Use, and Theory of Educational MOOs. Eds. Cynthia Haynes and Jan Rune Holmevik. 1998. Ann Arbor, MI: University of Michigan Press, 2001. 253–65.

Kolodny, Annette. "A Map for Rereading: Or, Gender and the Interpretation of Literary Texts." *The Captive Imagination: A Casebook on* The Yellow Wallpaper. Ed. Catherine Golden. New York: The Feminist Press, 1992. 149–67.

Murray, Janet H. *Hamlet on the Holodeck: The Future of Narrative in Cyberspace*. Cambridge, MA: MIT Press, 1997.

Peterson, Debra. MOO Space of Charlotte Perkins Gilman's "The Yellow Wallpaper." "The Yellow Wallpaper Estate." Connections MOO, 1 August 2000 <Telnet: connections.moo.mud.org:3333>.

Schöpp-Schilling, Beate. "'The Yellow Wallpaper': A Rediscovered 'Realistic' Story." *The Captive Imagination: A Casebook on* The Yellow Wallpaper. Ed. Catherine Golden. New York: The Feminist Press, 1992. 141–44.

Schweller, Ken. "MOO Educational Tools." *High Wired: On the Design, Use, and Theory of Educational MOOs*. Eds. Cynthia Haynes and Jan Rune Holmevik. 1998. Ann Arbor, MI: University of Michigan Press, 2001. 88–106.

Thomas, Heather Kirk. "'[A] Kind of 'Debased Romanesque' with *Delirium Tremens*': Late-Victorian Wall Coverings and Charlotte Perkins Gilman's 'The Yellow Wall-Paper.'" *The Mixed Legacy of Charlotte Perkins Gilman*. Eds. Catherine J. Golden and Joanna Schneider Zangrando. Newark: University of Delaware Press, 2000. 189–206.

Treichler, Paula A. "Escaping the Sentence: Diagnosis and Discourse in 'The Yellow Wallpaper'." *The Captive Imagination: A Casebook on* The Yellow Wallpaper. Ed. Catherine Golden. New York: The Feminist Press, 1992. 191–210.

Turkle, Sherry. "Foreword: All MOOs Are Educational—the Experience of 'Walking through the Self.'" *High Wired: On the Design, Use, and Theory of Educational MOOs*. Eds. Cynthia Haynes and Jan Rune Holmevik. 1998. Ann Arbor, MI: University of Michigan Press, 2001. ix–xix.

Joanne B. Karpinski

"I *WILL* FOLLOW THAT POINTLESS PATTERN"

A Formalist Approach to "The Yellow Wall-paper"

Judith Fetterley's "resisting reader" was a feminist who did not find herself represented in the major tropes of mainstream American literature. I find "resisting readers" of a different sort when I teach feminist literature three sorts, really: male students who do not find *them*selves represented in this kind of writing; more disturbingly, female students who believe that the issues raised by this literature have already been resolved and don't need to be hashed out yet again; and students of both genders, who, immune to the seductions of figurative language, suspect that the teacher is "reading in" levels of meaning beyond their experience.

When I teach "The Yellow Wall-paper" in an introduction to literature course, I frequently find that unsophisticated student readers are puzzled by the narrative tone and that they have a propensity to resolve their confusion by concluding, like John, that the narrator is simply deluded. But when the students engage in a formalist analysis of the text, they experience for themselves the defamiliarized environment within which the narrator discovers her secret sharer.

The formalist approach to literature focuses the reader's attention on the devices by which an author creates artistic effects and for this reason is somewhat neglected by contemporary theories that minimize the role of the individual author in the complex socio-cultural transactions through which literary meaning is communicated. Meta-literary theorizing necessarily relies on a thorough grounding in literary conventions; however, when teaching these conventions to students of lesser sophistication than literary theorists possess, I find that a formalist approach prepares the ground for exploring the ideological contours of a text. Although the first generation of formalists tended to regard a literary work as a closed system, the Bakhtin school linked the deployment of literary devices to the social context.

In his 1917 essay "Art as Technique," Viktor Shklovsky states that "the purpose of art is to impart the sensation of things as they are perceived and not as they are known. The technique of art is to make objects "unfamiliar" (Shklovsky 12). According to Shklovsky, the demands of everyday existence tend to "automatise" our responses to phenomena, but the artist can restore freshness of perception by interrupting our habituated reactions. Another formalist, Boris Tomashevsky, shows how the device of defamiliarization (*ostranenie* in Russian, literally "making strange") makes a political point in *Gulliver's Travels:*

> Compelled to tell everything with the utmost accuracy, [Gulliver] removes the shell of euphemistic phrases and fictitious traditions, which justify such things as war, class strife, parliamentary intrigue and so on. Stripped of their verbal justification and thus defamiliarised, these topics emerge in all their horror. (Tomashevsky 12)

These "euphemistic phrases and fictitious traditions which justify" can be understood as utterances by Bakhtin's "voice of the other," which an author "can also use [. . .] toward his own ends, in such a way that he imprints on this discourse, that already has, and keeps, its own orientation, a new semantic orientation [. . .]. A single discourse winds up having two semantic orientations, two voices" (Bakhtin 111). In some circumstances, however, the "voice of the other" may become so dominant that the voice of the author cannot reorient the discourse: "In especially unfavorable social conditions, such a cleavage between the person and the ideological environment that provides its nourishment can ultimately lead to the complete disintegration of consciousness, to disorder or insanity" (Voloshilov 71). The linguistic practices and their consequences described by Shklovsky, Tomashevsky, and Bakhtin can readily be discovered at work in "The Yellow Wall-paper."

It might be argued that a theoretical approach that assumes a conscious deployment of formal devices would be mooted by Gilman's own insistence that she was not a craftsman. Gilman claimed that the story was written in only two days, a torrid pace matched by the 103° weather in Pasadena at the time (*Diaries*, 905). As she told her second husband, "If you care little for my style why I care less—so there's no quarrel" (6 November 1898, qtd. in Hill, 198). In her autobiography, Gilman states that when William Dean Howells asked permission to include "The Yellow Wall-paper" in his 1920 anthology *Great Modern American Short Stories*, she "assured him that it was no more 'literature' than my other stuff" (*Living*, 121). However, as Nina Baym points out, many women writers of the nineteenth century "deliberately and even proudly disavowed membership in an artistic fraternity" (24), so Gilman's protestations need not be considered the last word on the subject. In addition, Gilman scholars generally consider "The Yellow Wall-paper" to be aesthetically superior to Gilman's typically utilitarian style.

Elaine Hedges, who reintroduced the story to contemporary readers, believes that "the story is narrated with clinical precision and aesthetic tact. The curt chopped sentences, the brevity of the paragraphs, which often consist of only one or two sentences, convey the taut, distraught mental state of the narrator. The style creates a controlled tension" (37). In the light of Gilman's well-known dislike of modernism, it may be overstatement on Catherine Golden's part to say that "Gilman may have called upon modernist techniques purposefully" (12), but she is correct in saying that the result of Gilman's stylistic decisions for "The Yellow Wall-paper" is "to show the narrator to be both fused with and distinct from the narrated much as she consciously shows the narrator to be separate from and joined with the woman trapped behind the wallpaper" (12). The confusion induced in the reader by this fusion in the text can be attributed to the action of another formalist device, *zatrudnenie* ("making difficult"), which forces the reader to slow down and pay sustained attention to the defamiliarized perspective of the narrative.

Gilman's primary strategy for defamiliarizing the narrative of "The Yellow Wall-paper" is to cross-pollinate two literary genres that the mainstream American literary tradition regards as incompatible: domestic fiction and the tale of terror. As Judith Fetterley points out, "Gilman opens her story with language evocative of Poe [. . .] here we have echoes of the 'scenes of mere household events' which the narrator of 'The Black Cat' wishes 'to place before the world'" (158). As happens frequently in Poe's tales, Gilman's narrative charts the gradual disintegration of a protagonist who, at the outset, seems ordinary enough, as do her surroundings: "although unusual perhaps, they are not extraordinary in the way Hawthorne's settings or Wilkie Collins' plots can be said to be extraordinary" (MacPike 286). Although she speaks of Gilman's contemporary readership, Annette Kolodny's diagnosis applies to today's students as well:

> As they had entered popular fiction by the end of the nineteenth century, however, the linguistic markers for those processes were at once heavily male-gendered and highly idiosyncratic, having more to do with individual temperament than with

> social or cultural situations per se [. . .]. Those fond of Poe could not easily transfer their sense of mental derangement to the mind of a comfortable middle-class wife and mother; and those for whom the woman in the home was a familiar literary character were hard-pressed to comprehend so extreme an anatomy of the psychic price she paid. (415)

Unable to rely fully on either set of genre conventions, the reader is forced to negotiate this defamiliarized literary landscape cautiously and attentively, replicating the protagonist's own determination to wrestle some meaning out of the inscrutable wallpaper:

> I determine for the thousandth time that I *will* follow that pointless pattern to some sort of a conclusion.
>
> I know a little of the principle of design, and I know this thing was not arranged on any laws of radiation, or alternation, or repetition, or symmetry, or anything else that I ever heard of. (34)

It is true that students who have not read a great deal of Poe or Hawthorne or any of Wilkie Collins novels, will have encountered the admixture of the domestic and the horrific in popular culture, in the books of Stephen King and films like the *Friday the Thirteenth* series. Their ability to negotiate the conventions of these works, however, may not be very helpful in coming to grips with the defamiliarization of the encounter in "The Yellow Wall-paper." In King's work as in the scary teen-flick subgenre, both the source of terror and the narrative point of view are external, and so the reader/viewer can establish a distanced perspective. The defamiliarization induced by "The Yellow Wallpaper" happens to the reader as well as to the character in the text and so is more difficult to reconcile.

Gilman's story is formally divided into undated diary-like entries, which typically break off when the narrator is about to be discovered at her forbidden work or when she is overwhelmed by sleep. Thus her life as a creative woman is suspended between the polarities of male authority and the claims of the unconscious. Judith Fetterley connects this women's situation to that of the female victims in Poe's tales of terror:

> Poe's ancestral halls/texts are haunted by the ghosts of women buried alive within them, hacked to death to produce their effect, killed by and in the service of the necessities of male art [. . .]. Written from the point of view of a character trapped in that male text—as if the black cat or Madeline Usher should actually find words and speak—Gilman's narrator shifts the center of attention away from the male mind that has produced the text and directs it instead to the consequences for women's lives of men's control of textuality. (164)

The success of this shift depends on the competence of the reading audience in negotiating the divergent literary conventions activated by the text and on its patience with the textual difficulties produced by this divergence. Since I can't be assured that my lower-division students have come to class fully equipped with either of these readerly virtues, I use the formalist method of "laying bare the device" (*obnazhenie priema*) to facilitate the necessary shift in perspective. I divide the class into small groups, each responsible for one section (or two of the very short sections) of the text. Within each group, individual students are responsible for listing all the narrator's descriptive terms for the house and its furnishings, for John, for the nursery, and, of course, for the wallpaper.

By developing a cumulative list of these descriptors during class discussion, students come to realize how early in the text the narrator perceives what she cannot acknowledge: that her "dream house" is the house of patriarchy, which has become a troubled, divisive inheritance; that the nursery is an infantilizing prison, a damaged asylum; that "dear John" exercises marital and medical authority to belittle her; that the wallpaper pattern not only imprisons but embodies deformed, festering, maddened and maddening, suicidally thwarted human (not specifically female) potential. They come to see the narrative tone as dialogical, simultaneously presenting and deconstructing the restrictive codes of turn-of-the-century marriage and motherhood. Their resistance to a feminist reading of the text (or a Marxist or a Lacanian one, I suppose, although I don't pursue these possibilities in a lower-division course) is reduced by their own acts of reading. They learn to perform what Laura Mulvey calls "feminist formalism" (qtd. in Naiman 335).

The narrator's descriptions of the house in which she finds herself figure forth her (and, significantly, John's) precarious position within the social order. They are "ordinary people," who "seldom secure ancestral halls" (29), even for a brief period. Paradoxically, they are renting "a hereditary estate" to which they do not claim a birthright; indeed, there appear to be *no* legitimate heirs to this structure. John reacts to the "felicity" of temporarily inhabiting "a colonial mansion" like a true subaltern, strenuously enforcing the hierarchy in order to reinforce his own slightly superior place within it and unwilling to make any alterations in the structure in order to accommodate his wife. The narrator rightly suspects that this edifice is flawed: "Else, why should it be let so cheaply?" (29). Beautiful but isolated, its "hedges and walls and gates that lock" (30) imprison the inhabitants as well as defend them from intruders. Nevertheless, the *hortus conclusus* has been violated—its greenhouses are already broken when the narrator moves in, and by the end of her tale the garden is filled by so many women creeping so fast that the narrator doesn't even want to look out the window at them.

When Huckleberry Finn can no longer tolerate the strictures of polite society, he lights out for the territories. But the narrator of "The Yellow Wall-paper" is not even allowed to have a room of her own (significantly, the room she desired had an outside entrance and a single bed). The narrator may admire the view of the "lovely shaded winding road" and the "lovely country, too, full of great elms and velvet meadows" (33), but as Janice Haney-Peritz observes, "In 'The Yellow Wall-paper,' the narrator does not move out into the open country"; instead, "she turns an ancestral hall into a haunted house and then encrypts herself therein as a fantasy figure" (128). Although she is able to liberate her double from the confines of the wallpaper, she becomes the agent of her own confinement by throwing away the key and tying herself to the gnawed bedstead. This self-interfering behavior mitigates the interpretation of the narrator as an icon of feminism and links her instead to the "Women of Today" that Gilman poetically chastises because "there is no hope until you dare to know/The thing you are!" (*Our World*, 128–9).

The room in which the narrator imprisons herself in order to liberate her double is one that she originally did not like a bit. Still, she attempts to put the best face possible on it, judging it to have been a nursery first, then a playroom, and then a gymnasium, thus assigning a nurturing and protective role to the bars on the windows, rings in the walls, and gate at the head of the stairs. Significantly, she accounts for the damage to the decor by imagining that this room served as a school for boys, a purpose indeed served by the social structure embodied by this hereditary estate, although her later actions suggest that the gnawed bedstead and stripped paper may be the work of another woman imprisoned there. In either case, she sees that "perseverance as well as hatred" (33) motivates violent retribution—scratching, gouging, splintering, digging, gnawing—against the confines of the structure. Ultimately, the narrator comes to think it fortunate that her baby is too well and happy to be confined as she is: "Why, I wouldn't have a child of mine, an impressionable little thing, live in such a room for worlds" (35). Perhaps her son can escape the nursery, but the boy's school and the gymnasium still await the children of patriarchy.

In 1923, University of Chicago professor Edith Foster Flint wrote to Gilman, seeking a definitive statement about the use to which the attic chamber had previously been put, since this was a point about which her students, and even she herself, remained in the dark. Gilman notes on Flint's letter that she replied "promptly and at length," but this reply has been lost (qtd. in Dock 97). But even without Gilman's authoritative interpretation, the textual descriptors speak for themselves. Loralee MacPike sums up the cumulative impact of these descriptions:

> The fact that the narrator's prison-room is a nursery indicates her status in society. The woman is legally a child; socially, economically, and philosophically she

> must be led by an adult—her husband; and therefore a nursery is the appropriate place to house her. The narrator's work threatens to destroy her status as a mere child by gaining her recognition in the adult world; this is reason enough for her husband to forbid her to work. Her work is, as he suggests, dangerous; but its danger is for him, not for her, because it removes her from his control. The nursery, then, is an appropriate symbol for the desired state of childlikeness vis-à-vis the adult world that her husband wishes to enforce. (288)

A certain number of my students would find MacPike's account unnecessarily sinister. Because the narrator's husband John is "a physician of high standing" (29), they are tempted to see the narrator's initial submission to his authority as legitimate in context and to exonerate John for the disastrous consequences of his treatment of her. However, paying careful attention to the narrator's descriptions of her husband undermines an assumption of reasonableness on his part. She writes that John is practical "in the *extreme*" (29) and has a "horror" of superstition; his apparent commitment to reason is irrationally maintained. He laughs at his wife, subjects her to a highly regulated infantile regime, and addresses her with belittling pet names that identify her with children or animals rather than with mature womanhood (a degrading habit he shares with Nora's husband in *A Doll's House*).

Like the protagonist of Nathaniel Hawthorne's "The Birthmark," John is revealed as a man of science, whose horror of the defective reflects his own failure of imagination. In both stories, the male authority figure's efforts to cure his wife, to create a perfect feminine image, destroy the real woman in the process. This commonality of plot connects to a central concern of nineteenth-century American literature, that an excessively pragmatic philosophy denies the value of the imagination. As Conrad Shumaker asks:

> What happens to the imagination when it's defined as feminine (and thus weak) and has to face a society that values the useful and the practical and rejects anything else as nonsense? [. . .] Imagination and art are subversive because they threaten to undermine his materialistic universe. Ironically, despite his abhorrence of faith and superstition, John fails because of his own dogmatic faith in empiricism. (599)

Although the narrator's imagination is devalued, it is not exterminated, but its subversive energy rebounds on the narrator who is forbidden to put it to work. Deprived of useful outlet, the narrator's imagination (which even John describes as a "power") obsessively focuses on the wallpaper. Her descriptions abound with verbal phrases that imbue the wallpaper with the vitality that she herself is not permitted to exercise. The first impact of this vitality is intellectual rather than physical: the wallpaper confuses, irritates, provokes, repels, and revolts. It commits every artistic sin and destroys itself in unheard-of contradictions, acting in demonic opposition to John's hyper-rationalism. It is drunk and impertinent, and looks as if "it *knew* what a vicious influence it had!" (32).

The narrator links this demonic consciousness to an infantile body, for she describes the pattern as having a lolling neck and bulbous eyes; it crawls and wallows around the room. "The new mother's description of the wallpaper evokes an image of an insatiable child who seems to be crawling everywhere," writes Jeffrey Berman (34). Not only insatiable, but violent—"it slaps you in the face, knocks you down, and tramples upon you" (37). Because the narrator also describes the pattern as "an interminable string of toadstools" (37), Berman also notes that "The wallpaper imagery evokes an appalling eruption of subhuman life, uncontrolled reproduction" (37), but my students tend to resist this move from the image of infancy to that of reproduction. Perhaps because a large number of my students come from polite Catholic households, it is more conventional for them to perceive (or at least to speak aloud about) the lurid color and sulphurous smell of the wallpaper as demonic emanations rather than as infantile defecations or sexual emissions, but once they have focused on the figurative possibilities of the wallpaper's color and smell, it becomes possible for me to bring into play other interpretative possibilities that propriety had repressed for them as it had for the narrator.

In the course of compiling the narrator's descriptors for the wallpaper, my students notice that they are not only abundant but also contradictory. It's an adult; it's an infant; it's a fungus; it's a debased artform, and "it changes as the light changes" (37). Taking notice of these descriptive contradictions leads the students to contemplate other irreconcilable features of the narrative that contribute to the effect of defamiliarization. At one point, the narrator imagines that the head of any woman who tries to climb through the pattern is strangled by it and turned into one of the many heads that figure in the wallpaper pattern. This fusion of the pattern and the woman trying to escape from it prefigures the disturbing fusion of the narrator with the figure imprisoned behind the wallpaper.

Even students who can accept the apparent teamwork between the "real" and the "imagined" woman encoded in the phrase "I pulled and she shook, I shook and she pulled" (40) nevertheless struggle with the apparent substitution by which the "real" woman looking out the window at all those creeping women wonders "if they all come out of that wall-paper as I did?" (41). They tend to interpret this fusion clinically, as evidence that John's diagnosis was correct. But based on their growing formalist consciousness, I can encourage them to look at this linguistic confusion as yet another device, an instance of figuration. As Kolodny points out, figurative language "often enough marks the highly specialized language of literature"; furthermore, it "is gender-sensitive to the extent that a male reader might have great difficulty in gaining access to and accurately interpreting women's conceptual and symbolic worlds" (431). At the same time, a language developed in order to grant access and accurate interpretation to *men's* conceptual and symbolic worlds might be an ineffective vehicle for the narrator's project.

Paula Treichler offers one explanation for how the narrator copes with this dilemma: "The narrator in 'The Yellow Wall-paper' initially speaks a language authorized by patriarchy, with genuine language ('work') forbidden her. But as the wallpaper comes alive she devises a different, 'impertinent' language, which defies patriarchal control and confounds the predictions of male judgment (diagnosis)" (323). Judith Fetterley also emphasizes the linguistic difference between the male and the female world view but is less sanguine about the prospect that a woman's voice can "confound the predictions of male judgment":

> Gilman works out in considerable detail the position [. . .] that in a sexist culture the interests of men and women are antithetical, and, thus, the stories each has to tell are not simply alternate versions of reality, they are rather, radically incompatible. The two stories cannot coexist; if one is accepted as true, then the other must be false, and vice versa. Thus the struggle for control of textuality is nothing less than the struggle for control over the definition of reality and hence over the definition of sanity and madness. (154)

This is a restatement, in feminist terms, of Bakhtin's previously cited observation that "in especially unfavorable social conditions, such a cleavage between the person and the ideological environment that provides its nourishment can ultimately lead to the complete disintegration of consciousness, to disorder or insanity" (Voloshilov 71).

This is the discursive situation that Luce Irigaray confronts when she asks, "How can women analyze their exploitation, inscribe their claims, within an order prescribed by the masculine?" She suggests that a woman might "play with mimesis": "resubmit herself to 'ideas,' notably about her, elaborated in/by a masculine logic" (qtd. in Haney-Peritz 123). Haney-Peritz notes that "In 'The Yellow Wall-paper,' the narrator's labor of miming does seem to produce just some such uncanny effect [as making visible what should have remained hidden]" (127). Such miming becomes parodic, in Tynianov's sense of the term; that is, an echoing that alters a statement, often by recontextualization, so that the original no longer serves its intended use (Naiman 344). Moreover, the narrative voice deals with the impasse between masculine logical discourse and the claims of female consciousness by breaking off at the point of impasse and jumping to another topic. This device, according to Haney-Peritz, can make the reader "aware of gaps in that discursive structure" (124). In creating a narrative texture that makes visible what would have remained hidden under ordinary discursive conditions and reveals the gaps in ordinary discursive structure, Gilman employs the formalist technique of "laying bare the device."

The formalist method suffered vigorous critique for Shklovsky's notorious statement that "Formalism is indifferent to the color of the flag flying over the fortress." But this is precisely its virtue for reaching students who are resistant to an ideological approach, who object that such a project involves "reading into the text" in a way that they suspect to be illegitimate. Indifferent does not mean inattentive; by focusing on formal structures, students find that values are imbedded in the language of the text, not imposed by the teacher. The deforming effect of patriarchy is exposed as the differential relationship between patriarchal discourse and the discourse of dawning feminist consciousness.

Works Cited

Bakhtin, Mikhail. *Problems of Dostoevsky's Poetics*. Trans. W.W. Rotsel. Ann Arbor: Ardis Press, 1973.

Baym, Nina. *Women's Fiction: A Guide to Novels by and About Women in America 1820–1870*. Ithaca, NY: Cornell University Press, 1978.

Berman, Jeffrey. "The Unrestful Cure: Charlotte Perkins Gilman and "The Yellow Wallpaper."" *The Talking Cure: Literary Representations of Psychoanalysis*. New York: New York University Press, 1985. 33–59.

Dock, Julie Bates, Comp. and Ed. *Charlotte Perkins Gilman's "The Yellow Wall-paper" and the History of Its Publication and Reception: A Critical Edition and Documentary Casebook*. University Park, PA: The Pennsylvania State University Press, 1998.

Fetterley, Judith. "Reading about Reading: 'A Jury of Her Peers,' 'The Murders in the Rue Morgue,' and 'The Yellow Wall-paper.'" *Gender and Reading: Essays on Readers, Texts and Contexts*. Eds. Elizabeth A. Flynn and Patrocinio Schweikert. Baltimore: Johns Hopkins University Press, 1986. 158–64.

Gilman, Charlotte Perkins. *The Diaries of Charlotte Perkins Gilman*. Ed. Denise D. Knight. Charlottesville, VA: University Press of Virginia, 1994.

——. *In This Our World*. 3rd ed. Boston: Small, Maynard, 1898.

——. *The Living of Charlotte Perkins Gilman*. Ed. Ann J. Lane. Madison: University of Wisconsin Press, 1991.

——. "The Yellow Wallpaper." 1892. *Charlotte Perkins Gilman's "The Yellow Wallpaper" and the History of Its Publication and Reception: A Critical Edition and Documentary Casebook*. Comp. and Ed. Julie Bates Dock. University Park, PA: The Pennsylvania State University Press, 1998. 29–42.

Golden, Catherine, Ed. *The Captive Imagination: A Casebook on* The Yellow Wallpaper. New York: The Feminist Press, 1992. 1–23.

Haney-Peritz, Janice. "Monumental Feminism and Literature's Ancestral House: Another Look at 'The Yellow Wall-paper,'" *Women's Studies* 12.2 (1986): 113–28.

Hedges, Elaine. "Afterword." *The Yellow Wallpaper*. Charlotte Perkins Gilman. Ed. Elaine Hedges. New York: The Feminist Press, 1973. 37–63.

Hill, Mary A. *A Journey from Within: The Love Letters of Charlotte Perkins Gilman*. Lewisburg, PA: Bucknell University Press, 1995.

Kolodny, Annette. "A Map for Rereading: Or, Gender and the Interpretation of Literary Texts." *New Literary History* 11.3 (1989): 415–41.

MacPike, Loralee. "Environment as Psychopathological Symbolism in 'The Yellow Wallpaper.'" *American Literary Realism, 1870–1910* 8.3 (1975): 286–88.

Naiman, Eric. "Shklovsky's Dog and Mulvey's Pleasure: The Secret Life of Defamiliarization." *Comparative Literature* 50.4 (Fall 1998): 333–52.

Shumaker, Conrad. "'Too Terribly Good To Be Printed': Charlotte Gilman's 'The Yellow Wallpaper.'" *American Literature* 57.4 (1985): 588–99.

Shklovsky, Victor. "Art as Technique." Rpt. in *Russian Formalist Criticism: Four Essays*. Trans. Lee T. Lemon and Marion J. Reis. Lincoln, NE: University of Nebraska Press, 1965.

Tomashevsky, Boris. "Theory of Parody." *A Reader's Guide to Contemporary Literary Theory*. Ed. Raman Selden. Lexington, KY: University of Kentucky Press, 1985.

Treichler, Paula. "Escaping the Sentence: Diagnosis and Discourse in 'The Yellow Wallpaper.'" *Tulsa Studies in Women's Literature* 4.2 (1985): 323–30.

Tynianov, Yuri. *Dostoevski and Gogol: Towards a Theory of Parody*. Letchworth, UK: Prideaux, 1985.

Voloshilov, V.N. "Stylistics of Discourse: 2. The Construction of Utterances." *Writings of the Circle of Bakhtin*. Trans. Wlad Godzich. Minneapolis: University of Minnesota Press, 1985.

Jonathan Crewe

QUEERING "THE YELLOW WALL-PAPER"

A Pedagogic View

The underlying conviction of this paper is that Charlotte Perkins Gilman's "The Yellow Wall-paper," already a notable teaching text in feminist and other contexts, lends itself to queer pedagogy at a college and even advanced high school level. [1] Below I will explain what I mean by queer pedagogy and why I believe "The Yellow Wall-paper" lends itself to that important yet still precarious and ill-defined task. At the start, however, I want to make it clear that I consider queer pedagogy both a responsibility and an opportunity for educators as such, not merely for people self-identified as queer. I deliberately do not say "humanities educators," since I do not believe that possibilities and responsibilities for queer pedagogy are absent from the sciences and social sciences, let alone from emerging interdisciplinary fields. My practical concern here is, however, with the humanities and especially with the educative potential of literary texts.

Pedagogic opportunity and responsibility flow from the achievements of modern criticism and scholarship in establishing queerness as anything but a marginal or incidental factor in cultural history. Despite a long history of efforts to associate queerness—and queer-identified people—with the trivial or the pernicious, queer energies can be traced in every sphere of cultural life and major cultural achievement. If nothing else, common honesty and scholarly integrity thus require the acknowledgment rather than continuing denial of queerness as a major element and shaping force in textual, hence cultural, production.

How individual educators choose to construe their responsibility or engage in queer pedagogy cannot, of course, be legislated. Educational contexts, teaching approaches, and even personal "comfort levels" will vary widely; so will local pressures of censorship and reprisal. Moreover, in the teaching process, queer considerations will not always be equally pertinent to the matter in hand. Yet acknowledging queerness and legitimizing the topic for students seem like the minimum general effort now incumbent on educators.

To say this is not to ignore the existence of professed educators for whom the denial or stigmatization of queerness figures as a moral calling rather than as a form of bigotry. Nor is it to ignore the coercive, often punitive, legislation of "family values" in the public and educational spheres. On the contrary, it is partly those persistent conditions that render the assumption of queer *educational* responsibility meaningful and even imperative. For those willing to assume the responsibility, it is not necessarily an impediment that queer pedagogy has been codified and institutionalized only to a limited degree in American higher education. As I will suggest below, any definitive codification of queer pedagogy would be problematic if not contradictory. So would the attempted formation of a distinctively queer canon: the point is that queerness does not exist apart from the "general culture" but rather belongs constitutively to it.

The relatively uncodified nature of queer pedagogy at present and in any foreseeable future leaves the field wide open to resourceful and inventive approaches. By the same token, potentialities for queer reading need to be explored, tested, and extended rather than dogmatically asserted. It is to this experimental process, in which teachers will necessarily remain learners at least as much as they are instructors, that I believe "The Yellow Wall-paper" strongly lends itself. What follows, therefore, is not a demonstration of how queer reading *should* be taught—not the demonstration of a sure-fire method—but rather an attempt to take on queer reading, hence queer teaching, as a challenge. Given both the difficulties and the forms of resistance confronting queer pedagogies in many schools and colleges, "The Yellow Wall-paper" commends itself, not just as an already widely taught canonical text but as a rich, engaging heuristic *exemplum*, perhaps above all for initiatory, non-confrontational queer teaching. The "mystery" of the protagonist's condition is one to which students might be invited to seek textual "clues," even if no reading, not even a queer one, should be proposed as a definitive solution.

Let us begin, then, by taking a step back into the recent critical history in which "The Yellow Wall-paper" emerged, first as a feminist classic and then as a generally admired canonical American text (a history in which Gilman's fortunes as an author rose correspondingly). Queer reading and teaching of "The Yellow Wall-paper" are not merely enabled by earlier feminist attention to this text but remain continuous in some respects with feminist pedagogy. That successive yet continuous relation between feminist and queer teaching does not obtain only in the case of "The Yellow Wall-paper." On the contrary, it is a relation that underwrites a good deal of queer pedagogy even when queer pedagogy works to de-essentialize the gender difference from which feminism takes its departure. Not just some possibilities of queer reading but this enabling relation can be brought into view in the classroom.

Briefly, then, the republication of Gilman's 1892 text by The Feminist Press in 1973—as an exemplary, counter-patriarchal text by a woman author—signified the militant entry of feminism into the American academy.[2] The retrieval of Gilman's work was part of a larger project to recover the work of neglected woman writers, yet "The Yellow Wall-paper" presented itself as a programmatic *feminist* text *par excellence*. In what did its exemplariness consist? Patriarchal oppression, as represented in Gilman's story, is not overtly cruel, lawless, or despotic—not overtly "Gothic," in other words—yet for that very reason the text peculiarly lent itself to academic feminist polemic, interpretation, and teaching. The economically privileged protagonist inhabits and writes within the social codes of educated, cultivated civility, a fact that made her a powerful identificatory figure for middle-class feminists.

The protagonist's mildly expressed discontents are treated by her doctor-husband as pathological symptoms. He subjects her to an ostensibly caring yet abjecting health regime in which male conjugal and medical authority fully coincide. The protagonist-speaker's predicament thus consists in finding both her subjectivity and her social critique always forestalled by a superior competent authority, both medical and conjugal. Barred as a woman from possessing such authority herself, the woman as wife-patient *ipso facto* cannot know what is best for her. Her resistance, always regarded by her husband as merely symptomatic, is invalidated in advance. The contemporary Weir Mitchell rest cure provides the immediate context for Gilman's novella,[3] yet that cure in turn evokes a long history in which women's social or political critiques were "treated" rather than credited.[4] That the gifted, articulate, imaginative "patient" is driven to solitary madness by her "kindly" treatment constituted the point for feminist critics seeking to dismantle the discursive and material conditions of the protagonist's subjection.

What gave "The Yellow Wall-paper" its peculiar force as a feminist exemplum was its "subjective" (first-person) narrative, couched from start to finish in the language of polite, civil rationality, of a progression culminating in madness. This fictional tour de force made Gilman's writer-protagonist a potent figure in feminist polemic, her cause being embraced by critics wishing to terminate an overlong historical succession of madwomen in the attic.[5] The fact that, in the narrative, the protagonist's room bears ominous traces of its former uses both as a schoolroom and a gymnasium establishes a social continuum among schooling, oppression, and madness. Disrupting that continuum became an important goal of feminist critics and educators. Insofar as Gilman's text became an instrument of academic change as well as a feminist proof-text, the protagonist's ultimately "bizarre" or "insane" vision was legitimized and rationalized by feminist critics *against* the apparatus of delegitimization deployed against the protagonist in the novella. In other words, the competence and legitimacy of the fictional husband's "treatment" of his wife came sharply into question as did its historical antecedents. What madness, readers were invited to ponder, possesses the husband to separate his wife from society, abandon her to herself for long periods of time, virtually incarcerate her under the surveillance of his sister, and deny her any mental occupation? What does it mean when *he* ends up "crying for an axe?"[6]

Even when second-guessing feminist critics backed away from full identification with the narrator's experience and perspective as that of oppressed Woman, rehabilitation of male conjugal-medical authority by no means followed. Instead, "The Yellow Wall-paper" remained, as it still does, a singularly challenging and rewarding text for nuanced feminist reading. Not only does Gilman's text reward the closest examination, thus offering itself as an important counter-patriarchal reading exercise, but it renders salient a social and literary history of women's psychotherapeutic "management" and its consequences. It thus continues to prompt historical and contextual inquiry. The present volume attests to the centrality of "The Yellow Wall-paper" in feminist (and other) pedagogy.[7]

All this being so, it remains to be added that the moment in which "The Yellow Wall-paper" seemed most definitively to capture the predicament of Woman was also the moment when a white middle-class feminism had yet to be confronted with painful differences of class, ethnicity, and global location among *women*. Moreover, it was the moment before gay and/or queer critiques of normative heterosexuality had seriously been pursued in the academy. Such critiques now having fully emerged, the question arises of "The Yellow Wall-paper"'s amenability to queer or queer-feminist reading and teaching. Can it hold its place as vital critical document in this context? I have already suggested that I believe it can.

I should add here that I choose the term "queer" advisedly rather than, for example, "gay." No one needs to be told that the term "queer" circulated (and continues to do so) in our culture as a term of prejudicial abuse directed against people perceived or self-identified as homosexual. The term thus defends an imagined heterosexual community and male-female heterosexual identities by seeking to abject and exclude those who are "different." More recently, however, the term "queer" has been appropriated by many who choose to identify themselves as queer and who pursue political and intellectual agendas designated as queer ones. The term "queer" has, in fact, largely superseded both "gay" and "homosexual" as a term of self-identification. "Gay" tends to reinforce the notion that some people are predestined to a homosexual identity or sexual orientation, while others are predestined to a heterosexual one. It then follows that "gay" literature, for example, will merely reflect (or project) this pre-existing disposition. "Homosexual," on the other hand, is a historically recent term, having been coined only in the nineteenth century as part of a larger project to classify and hence control varieties of sexual behavior. In fixing the homosexual as a pathological type, nineteenth-century sexology also established the cultural identity of "the homosexual" as distinct. Same-sex attractions and behaviors had not previously been fixed in this way. Reading "homosexuality" back into earlier periods thus became a serious and widely practiced form of historical misrepresentation.

What has come to be called queer theory goes well beyond both "gay studies" and "homosexual" advocacy. It does not assume fixed, innate sexual identities or dispositions, let alone ones capable of being reduced to the simple alternatives of homo- and hetero-. On the contrary, queer theory challenges this sexual binarism, calling for a rethinking of sexuality across a broad spectrum that includes various forms of heterosexuality. It challenges as well any assumption that cultural products, including works of literature, simply follow from one or other sexual "identity." Finally, without disputing that cultural desire and practice are constantly and profoundly informed by their sexual counterparts, queer theory nevertheless challenges any simple causality linking one to the other.

We might then say, following Eve Kosofsky Sedgwick, that queering "The Yellow Wall-paper" would mean more than just identifying a homoerotic subtext or mode of repressed desire in it. It would at least include the continuing process of tracking "the *gravitas*, the meaning, but also the center of gravity [as] the term 'queer' itself [historically] deepens and shifts" (*Tendencies*, xii).[8] Sedgwick adds: "'queer' can refer to [. . .] the open mesh of possibilities, gaps, overlaps, dissonances, resonances, lapses, and excesses of meaning when the constituent elements of anyone's gender, or anyone's sexuality aren't made (or *can't* be made) to signify monolithically" (*Tendencies*, 9). Both queer sexuality and queer reading are unfixed, always in process, always resisting cultural or political pressures to make things "signify monolithically."

It is in the context created by queer theory that many "queer" features of "The Yellow Wall-paper" call for attention. As if by uncanny coincidence or historical anticipation, the term "queer" and such cognates as "strange" and "peculiar" (both of which have done duty as socially stigmatizing euphemisms for the homosexual) circulate prominently in "The Yellow Wall-paper." I know of no study that definitively connects "queerness" to same-sex attraction or practice before 1922, when "queer" was first cited as a colloquial term for the male homosexual in the *OED*.[9] However, the circulation and resonances of the term in late-nineteenth and early-twentieth-century texts—not just Gilman's—now solicit attention, especially in contexts of marked "strangeness" or social anomalousness. The "new" sense of the term could not have emerged punctually in 1922, its arrival immediately heralded by the *OED*.

The "queer" experience of the narrator in "The Yellow Wall-paper," including her projective-defensive relation to the wallpaper, gets implicitly connected to a scenario of repressed desire in the text. This desire might be called "lesbian," implying an inadmissible positive orientation, but might equally be recognized as a desire constitutively repressed under what Adrienne Rich famously called the regime of compulsory heterosexuality. The narrator's disaffection from her husband and phobic relation to her child ("Such a dear baby! And yet I *cannot* be with him, it makes me so nervous" [31]) as well as her partial transfer of affection to the "sister" Jennie—husband's sibling-surrogate, other woman, sister-in-law, nursing-sister, keeper—are consistent with this oppressive regime. The norm of conjugal, heterosexual maternity in which the protagonist as mother finds herself situated is both infantilizing and desexualizing; it mandates the nursery for the mother as well as the infant. The narrator's "discovery" of a woman, and a queer one at that, in the wallpaper patterns that fascinate her constitutes a form of (self-)recognition.[10] Under the conditions that prevail in the novella, however, this "private" recognition remains inseparable from madness. It can find no place in public discourse.

Proceeding more deductively now, let us consider some of the manifestations of queerness in "The Yellow Wall-paper." Gilman establishes a norm of rational civility and "ordinariness" both in the form of the novella and in the diction of its characters. No linguistic lapse or grammatical breakdown marks the narrator's apparent descent into terminal dementia unless her curious, incipiently vulgar, use of the term "smooches," by which critics have been puzzled, counts as a betraying lapse.[11] Part of the "The Yellow Wall-paper"'s power as well as much of its irony comes from the increasing discrepancy between normal genteel speech codes of the protagonist and the aberrant "social" actions or situations to which they refer. On one hand, this discrepancy attests to the protagonist's wish to make ordinary civil speech answerable to *her* subjectivity rather than oppressive of it; on the other hand, it dramatizes the widening gap in the novella between a public domain of ostensibly civil rationality and a private one of anguished subjectivity:

> To jump out of the window would be admirable exercise, but the bars are too strong even to try. (Gilman 41)

Despite their evidently bizarre content, the sentences late in the story are no less poised, lapidary, and decorous than the early ones:

> Now he's crying for an axe.
> It would be a shame to break down that beautiful door! (42)

> Now why should that man have fainted? But he did, and right across my path by the wall, so that I had to creep over him every time! (42)

The impersonal, neuter pronoun "one," in which, at first, the narrator submerges herself whenever her "I" thinks flighty or rebellious thoughts, is the pronoun that designates well-disciplined, class-marked, code-governed social personhood: "And what can one do?" "What is one to do?" (29). Mere personal opinion, whim, rebellion, or transgressive desire are strongly preempted by the coercively rational understandings and prohibitions embodied in the neuter pronoun:

> Personally, I disagree with their ideas.
> Personally, I believe that congenial work, with excitement and change, would do me good.
> But what is one to do? (29)

Any rebellion or deviancy is not only doomed, it would seem, but can manifest itself only as childishness, irrationality, or bad form.

Although the impersonal "one" soon disappears from the narrator's speech and the subjective "I" takes over, the narrator stringently maintains the social speech codes of decorous rationality in a (failing) effort to legitimize *her* increasingly "insane" view of things. Admittedly, the narrator may unconsciously be seeking refuge in madness. She may likewise "choose" the social space of the asylum, a domestic version of which she constructs in double-bind complicity with her handlers. Yet her normalizing (and self-normalizing) conditioning does not break down. On the contrary, it is maintained even as, with reference to prevailing norms, her thoughts become wilder, her subjectivity more perverse, her social perceptions more paranoid, her fantasies more "improperly" violent and sexualized, and her meanings less socially anchored and regulated. In short, normative language and perception are increasingly "queered"—rendered strange—by a narrator who indulges her subjectivity yet also feels threatened in her normality by doing so:

> There are things in that paper that nobody knows but me, or ever will.
> Behind that outside pattern the dim shapes get clearer every day.
> It is always the same shape, only very numerous.
> And it is like a woman stooping down and creeping about behind that pattern. I don't like it a bit. I wonder—I begin to think—I wish John would take me away from here! (35)

Knowledge experienced as wholly secret and unshareable, dimly apprehended "things," an outline growing clearer every day, the "shape" of a woman yet perhaps of all women, wondering, beginning to think: such are the components of a decidedly queer experience, yet one so immediately threatening to this self-styled ordinary person (29) that the repudiated husband has to be recalled as censor and heterosexual rescuer. The narrator's prissy "I don't like it a bit" sounds both genteel and regressively child-like. Yet without any conscious recourse, let alone political recourse, to same-sex desire or "sisterly" bonding, the narrator's queerness is mainly doomed to manifest itself perversely, symptomatically, self-destructively.

The narrator views her sister-in-law, "such a dear girl as she is" (33), preemptively as a conjugal collaborator, enforcer, and rival claimant upon the wallpaper (normalizing reader of it). She is thus on the other side, and her advances must always be regarded as devious:

> Jennie wanted to sleep with me—the sly thing!—but I told her I should undoubtedly rest better for a night all alone.
>
> That was clever, for really I wasn't alone a bit! As soon as it was moonlight and that poor thing began to crawl and shake the pattern, I got up and ran to help her.
>
> I pulled and she shook, I shook and she pulled, and before morning we had peeled off yards of that paper. (40)

Closing out the solicitous Jennie as bedfellow, the narrator assumes her caring role by becoming solicitous for the "poor thing" imprisoned behind the wallpaper. She then effects a chiastic interchange *with* that projected, imprisoned figure—"I pulled, and she shook, I shook and she pulled"—thus at once becoming her own liberator and female accomplice. Perhaps she is also precipitating something implied in the ordinary phrase "Jennie wanted to sleep with me."[12] Yet the narrator can envisage no benign sociopolitical translation (social realization) of her interior drama. If this incapacity attests to the prohibitive force of contemporary ideological "schooling," it nevertheless implies a certain tragic internalization on the part of the narrator as well: "what is one to do?"

When the narrator has stripped off much of the wallpaper with the imagined help of the "poor thing" she has freed, we hear that, on her return, the sister-in-law:

> [. . .] laughed and said she wouldn't mind doing it herself, but I must not get tired (41).

The narrator's proprietary, self-isolating relation to the wallpaper forecloses whatever she might have shared with this "sister" who so unexpectedly (and uniquely in this text) laughs before adding that she wouldn't mind doing it herself; that moment of laughter is one of potential freedom and solidarity.

The heavy loading of "queer" (strange, peculiar) in "The Yellow Wall-paper" seems, as I have already suggested, to anticipate the semantic shifts through which "queer" first becomes a pejorative colloquialism for the male homosexual as "deviant" and is subsequently extended to cover the entire same-sex field. No doubt "The Yellow Wall-paper" seems to anticipate subsequent developments because we can now read back repressed homoerotic desire into a text formally innocent of any such thing. Yet the text's insistence on queerness and its ramifications calls for recognition in its own right, and that insistence also summons up the range of significations to which Sedgwick has connected, not a reified "homosexuality" but a play of desire and identification within and against any prevailing norms—including aesthetic ones. Moreover, "The Yellow Wall-paper" situates the narrator's queerness—or, rather, its etiology—in a richly overdetermined context.

The first intimation of an unlocated queer craving or tendency is articulated in the third sentence of the "The Yellow Wall-paper." With the light, regulative irony "one" uses to admit a foible, the narrator, a self-declared ordinary person, says:

> Still I will proudly declare that there is something queer about it. (29)

What is queer? About what? Here are the antecedent sentences:

> IT is very seldom that mere ordinary people like John and myself secure ancestral halls for the summer.
>
> A colonial mansion, a hereditary estate, I would say a haunted house, and reach the height of romantic felicity—but that would be asking too much of fate! (29)

So what is queer? About what? No clear referent for "queer" or antecedent for "it" is pinned down in these sentences. Only in the sentence succeeding the narrator's timidly proud declaration does this narrowing specification seem to occur. "Else, why should it be let so cheaply?" This sentence establishes the house as the antecedent of "it." The queer situation is then the one in which a large house, classified in rapid succession as "ancestral hall, colonial mansion, hereditary estate," stands untenanted and has apparently done so for a long time as we learn in the next sentence.

Is it queer only, as the narrator seems to think, that a habitation so romantically desirable and so cheap should stand untenanted? Or is it queer, as we may think, that this so determinedly ordinary person should be susceptible to the stereotypical Gothic appeal of the ancestral hall and colonial mansion (not yet knowing what she is letting herself in for)? Is it already queer that she may be susceptible—more than she knows?—to whatever unnameable yet haunting forms of romantic felicity these locales intimate to her? Or is it really *not* so queer that one conscious of herself as ordinary—as an anonymous social cipher—should be susceptible to precisely these (literary) fantasies of the extraordinary? And really *not* so queer that others of her ordinary kind, perhaps more effectively schooled than she, should be aware of the socioeconomic reasons why a dysfunctionally large house stands untenanted? From the reader's perspective, in short, this situation may well seem less queer than it does to the narrator. Yet the narrator's unwary solicitation of the queer propels both her and the reader willy-nilly into further, defamiliarizing confrontation with queerness.

The narrator's initial invocation of queerness persists through a skeptical process in which banal causes are successively eliminated:

> There were greenhouses, too, but they are all broken now.
>
> There was some legal trouble, I believe, something about the heirs and coheirs; anyhow, the place has been empty for years.
>
> That spoils my ghostliness, I am afraid, but I don't care—there is something strange about the house—I can feel it. (30)

Queer, strange. Not the house but something about the house, pervasive yet still unlocated. Or about the narrator. Without ever being fully explained or decoded in the narrative, the narrator's projection of queerness eventually finds its objective correlative in the yellow wallpaper.

The first sentence that refers to the wallpaper shows how the wallpaper comes to stand (in) for whatever it is that elicits queer affect:

> It is stripped off—the paper—in great patches [. . .]. (30–31)

Characteristically, the referent comes after, not before, the pronoun.

The process of attachment begins offhandedly, the wallpaper being parenthetically introduced as one item among others in the room:

> It is stripped off—the paper—in great patches all around the head of my bed, about as far as I can reach, and in a great place on the other side of the room low down. I never saw a worse paper in my life.
>
> One of those sprawling flamboyant patterns committing every artistic sin.
>
> It is dull enough to confuse the eye in following, pronounced enough to constantly irritate and provoke study, and when you follow the lame uncertain curves for a little distance they suddenly commit suicide—plunge off at outrageous angles, destroy themselves in unheard of contradictions.
>
> The color is repellant, almost revolting; a smouldering unclean yellow, strangely faded by the slow-turning sunlight.
>
> It is a dull yet lurid orange in some places, a sickly sulphur tint in others.
>
> No wonder the children hated it! I should hate it myself if I had to live in this room long. (30–31)

The attachment of queer affect to the wallpaper presents itself as an attempted violent *detachment* from it on the part of the narrator, as if the connection were a frighteningly instantaneous, overwhelming or unsuspected preexisting one.

This peculiarity is partly accounted for, in historical terms, by Lutz's valuable observation (221–23) that the exasperating effect of patterned wallpaper on invalids was a medical commonplace of Gilman's time. As Robert W. Edis wrote in 1883: "The endless multiplication and monotony of strongly-marked [wallpaper] patterns [. . . is] a source of infinite torture and annoyance in times of sickness and sleeplessness" (Lutz 230). Lutz continues: "Not only did patterned wallpapers fail all aesthetic tests, but they could materially add to our discomfort and nervous irritability, and after a time have a ghastly and nightmarish effect on the brain" (230). Gilman thus apparently lines herself up with received (male) medical opinion in representing the highly irritating effect of the wallpaper on her invalid-protagonist; by the same token, the narrator's violent reaction to the wallpaper is not wholly bizarre or arbitrary, as it might now appear, but anticipated and "understood" in the contemporary discourse of neuraesthenia. (Gilman's fictionalization of this medical commonplace supports Lutz's general view that, as a writer, she is always positioned within the discourse of neuraesthenia, to which she gives substantial credence.) Yet Gilman's fictional incorporation of that medical discourse does not simply legitimize or reproduce it but resituates it in a highly overdetermined aesthetic and fictional context.

The narrator's outburst about the wallpaper is almost literally that: her diatribe bursts out of a parenthesis in a normal sentence, and out of a realist inventory of items in the room, with a negative intensity and hyperbolic energy that overtax these studiously ordinary grammatical and rhetorical forms. A dangerous intensification and breakout of this kind are partly anticipated and wishfully forestalled in the medical prose that itself speaks with gothic extravagance of wallpaper as a source of "infinite torture" and "a ghastly and nightmarish effect on the brain." Sociocultural norms, including ones of fictional realism, are clearly being defended under a supposedly caring, patient-centered, therapeutic regime. The narrator's outburst goes beyond codified, banal gothic, however, to constitute the yellow wallpaper as an objective correlative enabling a queer affect to be precipitated with vertiginous horror, strangeness, unbridled intensity, and barely admissible excitement.

The fact that the wallpaper is "committing every artistic sin"—the medical opinion thus being reaffirmed—now serves as permission to enumerate these sins glowingly rather than as a prohibition on any upsetting confrontation with them. It also enables a historic lexicon of aesthetic and art-historical denunciation to be incorporated, with visual examples, into "The Yellow Wallpaper." These strictures powerfully summon up perverse, non-realist energies, forms, and impulses of artistic production against which social and ideological norms have historically defended, not least during the *fin-de-siècle* period of Gilman's writing: "flamboyant," "dull," "lame," "uncertain," "outrageous," "unheard of," "repellant," "revolting," "lurid," "sickly," "vicious," "impertinen[t]," "bulbous," "absurd," "bloated," "debased," "fat[uous]," "sprawling," "grotesque," "lack[ing]," "defian[t]," "irritant to a normal mind," "torturing," "florid," "flourish[ing]," "arabesque," "interminable," "endless," "it gets in . . . my hair." Queerness in more than one sense is strongly implied in a number of these stigmatizing epithets; transverse orientations and violent distortions are particularly conspicuous in the wallpaper design.

When regulative principles of good form *are* stipulated by the narrator as art critic, they are not only introduced in the suspect guise of hearsay but constitute the wallpaper as a veritable field of energetic, whimsical, decorative flagrancy:

> I know a little of the principle of design, and I know this thing was not arranged on any laws of radiation, or alternation , or repetition, or symmetry, or anything else that I ever heard of.
>
> It is repeated, of course, by the breadths, but not otherwise.
>
> Looked at in one way each breadth stands alone, the bloated curves and flourishes—a kind of "debased Romanesque" with *delirium tremens*—go waddling up and down in isolated columns of fatuity.
>
> But, on the other hand, they connect diagonally, and the sprawling outlines run off in great slanting waves of optic horror, like a lot of wallowing sea-weeds in full chase. (34)

Whatever the immediate source of the narrator's neoclassical principles of symmetry, she experiences the irregularities of the wallpaper—or are they unintelligible and uncodifiable regularities?—as unfixed "waves of optic horror." Yet they evidently have their natural counterpart, not in the cultivated garden outside (itself progressively absorbed into the room as inside/outside boundaries break down in the narrator's mind) but in undulating seaweed. The sheer enumeration of these *apparent* irregularities, still ostensibly within the descriptive code of nineteenth-century domestic realism, infuses the narrator-writer's prose with an energetic brio, scathing intensity, and figurative extravagance foreign to the ordinary person, to ordinary prose.

If, then, Gilman as author is reinforcing the normalizing medico-aesthetic discourse of neuraesthenia, she is also, in effect, reversing its intent by making it the revelatory medium of the culturally perverse, extravagant, surreal, and vital. However "torturing," the narrator may find the wallpaper, it gives her perverse access to *pleasure* as well as compulsion in writing. As she acknowledges:

> I'm getting really fond of the room in spite of the wall-paper. Perhaps *because* of the wall-paper. (34)

As an "irritant," the wallpaper also paradoxically "provokes study" on the part of the narrator. This pleasurable torture ("No wonder the children hated it!" [31]) turns the sick room back into the classroom she has hitherto only imagined. In it, the narrator can apparently for the first time pursue an adult self-education as distinct from the blandly normative schooling in which her doctor-husband persists by denying her the "irritants" of strenuous reading and writing.

Neither "The Yellow Wall-paper"'s disturbing range of cultural and political implication nor the narrator's animated deviancy can be reduced to her "pathology" although psychoanalytic feminists have rightly cautioned against uncritical feminist identification with the protagonist. The drastic impasse represented in "The Yellow Wall-paper" is the sociocultural one in which the narrator's queer cognition, sensibility, and self-instruction are inseparable—practically indistinguishable—from symptoms of a "nervous breakdown." Reduced to a solitary, hystericized "I" following her catastrophic loss of the social personhood designated by the pronoun "one," the narrator substitutes paranoid self-scrutiny for social surveillance, and she is further threatened by an ego-depleting outflow into the room and its objects:

> There is a recurrent spot where the pattern lolls like a broken neck and two bulbous eyes stare at you upside down.
>
> [. . .] those absurd, unblinking eyes are everywhere. (32)

Attempting to defend against her new vulnerability to the temptation and threat of free fall, culminating in "sudden [. . .] suicide," "a broken neck," "headlong plunges of equal distraction," the narrator tries to recover the supposedly safe, healing ground of childhood fantasy:

> I remember what a kindly wink the knobs of our big, old bureau used to have, and there was one chair that always seemed like a strong friend.
>
> I used to feel that if any of the other things looked too fierce I could always hop into that chair and be safe. (32–33)

Far from saving the narrator, this nostalgic regression merely retraces her adult experience to a childhood already strange, solitary, and fiercely threatening. Her attempt to implicate the reader represents a failing—even comically failing—attempt to normalize her own condition: "we all know how much expression [inanimate things] have!" (32). If "we" do indeed know this, we have in all likelihood repressed it as an ego-threatening form of consciousness, thus making the narrator's appeal seem all the more "queer" or eccentric. We the readers are thus likely to find ourselves positioned as normal with respect to the narrator's deviancy, despite her attempts to interpellate us as participants in her singular narrative and her community of one. Yet if we cannot assent to incorporation in the narrator's "we," the force of her appeal and the anguish of her predicament may nevertheless instill a new self-consciousness regarding "our" sociohistorical positioning and political choices with respect to hers. Where, in effect, are *we* placed, or do *we* place ourselves and with what consequences for ourselves and others? If queer reading of "The Yellow Wallpaper" is tantamount to outing the narrator, no less is it tantamount in the end to outing the reader.

By producing this heuristic rebound on the reader, both "The Yellow Wallpaper" and its "mad" protagonist lend themselves strongly to a queer pedagogy directed not just towards textual interpretation but historical understanding and social change. To read this text as a "queer" one requires us both to move outside the text into the cultural history in which it is embedded *and* to recognize ourselves as the desperate protagonist's ultimate addressees. Such is the pedagogy, modeled by "The Yellow Wall-paper," that I take to be everybody's business, not only the business of, for example, self-identified queer feminists.

Notes

1. This essay is a thematically revised and updated version of one previously published. See Crewe.
2. The history of "The Yellow Wall-paper"'s initial publication and subsequent obscur-

ity, followed by revival in 1973, is extensively retold by Catherine Golden (*Captive Imagination*, 1992). See also Dock.

3. One very particular reader targeted by Gilman was Dr. S. Weir Mitchell himself, named in the text (30), to whose rest cure Gilman had submitted for three months in 1887 after a diagnosis of neuraesthenia and postpartum depression. Having heard a report that Mitchell had changed his infantilizing therapy after reading "The Yellow Wall-paper," of which Gilman had sent him a copy, Gilman remarked "If that is a fact, I have not lived in vain." This story and its ramifications have been extensively discussed by feminist critics. (See Golden in *Captive*, 7–8 and *passim*.)
4. Pertinent feminist essays or excerpts in *The Captive Imagination* include ones by Deirdre English, Ann Douglas Wood, Sandra Gilbert and Susan Gubar, Paula A. Treichler, and Jeffrey Berman. The pertinence of both the medical and juridical senses of the word "case" to *The Captive Imagination* as a feminist critical "casebook" is striking. The juridical aspect of the fictional situation as well as the reader's being called upon to render a verdict is discussed by Fetterley. See also Knight and Veeder. On the rest cure in the context of late-nineteenth-century "neuraesthenia," see, among others, Lutz and Will. The historical fact that Gilman suffered from postpartum depression has often been read into "The Yellow Wall-paper" by feminist critics, who assume that the narrator is likewise afflicted, but this naming of her condition drastically reduces the story's field of implication even if it helps to de-idealize maternity.
5. In her discussion of aristocratic women poets in the seventeenth century in *A Room of One's Own*, Virginia Woolf may have been the first modern feminist to see isolation and madness as a threatening, regular outcome of women's aspiration to become writers in a patriarchal culture. The point was, of course, elaborated by Gilbert and Gubar.
6. The husband's sanity is called into question by Fetterley.
7. For a survey of feminist responses to "The Yellow Wall-paper," criss-crossed by theoretical developments of the past three decades, see Hedges. Two notable moments of "withdrawal" are those enacted by Jacobus and Lanser. Jacobus cautions against hysterical reading and identification on the part of feminists and offers a qualified rehabilitation of Freud's diagnostic categories. Lanser recontextualizes Gilman's narrative in the "yellow peril" ideological climate of the 1890s, characterizing the protagonist, for all her proto-feminism, as an anxiously genteel, beleaguered, white middle-class woman, whose precarious subjectivity is constituted mainly with respect to the racialized rather than the gendered Other.
8. To a significant degree, the historical and interpretive premises of queer theory have been supplied by Michel Foucault. Much of what follows in my summary depends on Foucault's key argument that "the homosexual" is a creation of nineteenth-century sexology. See also Sedgwick, "The Beast in the Closet."
9. Quoted from a U.S. Labor Department report. The next citation, from G. Irwin, *Amer. Tramp & Underworld Slang* in 1931, importantly specifies "*effeminate* or degenerate men or boys" [my emphasis]. Widespread 1950s usage appears to have restricted the term to "effeminate men" and/or male transvestites." The first *OED* citation for "queer" as applied to women dates from 1974. In H. L. Mencken's historical survey of the American language, "queer" is cited twice in colloquial senses but never with the meaning "homosexual."
10. Following Gilbert and Gubar and Jacobus, it is possible to identify the "creeping" women hallucinated by the narrator as avatars of the sexualized-bestialized mad wife in *Jane Eyre*, yet neo-Darwinian fears of regression and degeneration may also come into

play in "The Yellow Wall-paper." As Gilbert and Gubar note, Gilman's version of the madwoman in the attic clearly belongs to the tradition of women's writing canonically inaugurated by *Jane Eyre*.

11. Jacobus comments on "smooches" as "the unsayable in Gilman's story—the sexual etiology of hysteria [. . .] but also the repression imposed by the 1890s on the representation of female sexuality, and, in particular, the repression imposed on women's writing" (288–89).

12. Dijkstra indicates that once-idealized female friendship comes under heavy misogynist suspicion for its "hidden" lesbian content in the late nineteenth century, while a certain ability to reappropriate the misogynist trope of the mannish/man-hating lesbian is evident in *fin-de-siècle* women's culture (64–82; 147–159).

Works Cited

Crewe, Jonathan. "Queering *The Yellow Wallpaper:* Charlotte Perkins Gilman and the Politics of Form." *Tulsa Studies in Women's Literature* 14 (Fall 1995): 273-93.

Dijkstra, Bram. *Idols of Perversity*. New York: Oxford University Press, 1986.

Dock, Julie Bates, Comp. and Ed. *Charlotte Perkins Gilman's "The Yellow Wall-paper" and the History of Its Publication and Reception: A Critical Edition and Documentary Casebook.* University Park, PA: The Pennsylvania State University Press, 1998.

Fetterley, Judith. "Reading about Reading: 'A Jury of her Peers,' 'The Murders in the Rue Morgue,' and 'The Yellow Wall-paper.'" *The Captive Imagination: A Casebook on* The Yellow Wallpaper. Ed. Catherine Golden. New York: The Feminist Press, 1992. 253–61.

Foucault, Michel. *The History of Sexuality: Volume 1*. New York: Pantheon, 1978.

Gilbert, Sandra M., and Susan Gubar. *The Madwoman in the Attic: The Woman Writer and the Nineteenth Century Literary Imagination*. New Haven: Yale University Press, 1979.

Gilman, Charlotte Perkins. "The Yellow Wallpaper." 1892. *Charlotte Perkins Gilman's "The Yellow Wall-paper and the History of Its Publication and Reception: A Critical Edition and Documentary Casebook*. Comp. and Ed. Julie Bates Dock. University Park, PA: The Pennsylvania State University Press, 1998. 29–42.

——. *The Yellow Wallpaper*. "Afterword." Elaine R. Hedges. New York: The Feminist Press, 1973.

Golden, Catherine, Ed. *The Captive Imagination: A Casebook on* The Yellow Wallpaper. New York: The Feminist Press, 1992.

——. "One Hundred Years of Reading "The Yellow Wallpaper." *The Captive Imagination: A Casebook on* The Yellow Wallpaper. Ed. Catherine Golden. New York: The Feminist Press, 1992. 1–23.

Hedges, Elaine R. "'Out at Last?': 'The Yellow Wallpaper' after Two Decades of Feminist Criticism." *The Captive Imagination: A Casebook on* The Yellow Wallpaper. Ed. Catherine Golden. New York: The Feminist Press, 1992. 319–33.

Jacobus, Mary. "An Unnecessary Maze of Sign-Reading." *The Captive Imagination: A Casebook on* The Yellow Wallpaper. Ed. Catherine Golden. New York: The Feminist Press, 1992. 277-95.

Knight, Denise. "The Reincarnation of Jane: 'Through This'—Gilman's Companion to 'The Yellow Wallpaper'." *Women's Studies* 20, 3–4 (1992): 287–302.

Lanser, Susan. "Feminist Criticism: 'The Yellow Wallpaper' and the Politics of Color in America." *Feminist Studies* 15, 3 (1989): 415–41.

Lutz, Tom. *American Nervousness, 1903: An Anecdotal History*. Ithaca: Cornell University Press, 1991.

Mencken, H. L. *The American Language: An Inquiry into the Development of English in the United States*. New York : A. A. Knopf, 1938.

Sedgwick, Eve Kosofsky. *Tendencies*. Durham, NC: Duke University Press, 1993.

——. "The Beast in the Closet: James and the Writing of Homosexual Panic." *Sex, Politics, and Science in the Nineteenth-Century Novel*. Ed. Ruth Bernard Yeazell. Baltimore: The Johns Hopkins University Press, 1986. 148–86.

Veeder, William. "Who Is Jane? The Intricate Feminism of Charlotte Perkins Gilman." *Arizona Quarterly* 44, 3 (Autumn 1988): 41–79.

Will, Barbara. "The Nervous Origins of the American Western." *American Literature* 70:2 (June 1998): 293–316.

Woolf, Virginia. *A Room of One's Own*. San Diego: Harcourt Brace Jovanovich, 1989.

Robyn Shaw

TEACHING "THE YELLOW WALL-PAPER" AND EXISTENTIALISM IN THE CLASSROOM

Though the relationship between existential philosophy and some works of twentieth-century fiction has been studied extensively, virtually no criticism has examined nineteenth-century supernatural fiction from an existential point of view. Thus, because of a clearly relevant connection, this chapter will focus upon Charlotte Perkins Gilman's "The Yellow Wall-paper" (1892) as an example of nineteenth-century supernatural fiction that invites existential analysis and hence also pedagogical re-evaluation.

An unfortunate but too often tacit assumption in teaching "The Yellow Wall-paper" is the student-reader should study the narrator, whom I will refer to as Jane for reasons explained below, from a distance as a subject of nineteenth-century brutality and sexism. However, as contemporary America is deeply concerned not only with issues of sexuality and power control but also of dysfunctional families, such distance seems unnecessary. Indeed, at a point in American history when divorce affects 40 to 50 percent of families, understanding husband and wife relationships has become increasingly important to developing teens. Thus, asking colleges students, "What difference does 'The Yellow Wall-paper' make to your life?" immediately identifies the link between the text and contemporary America. However, such a question is only the starting point.

Within the machinery of Gilman's nineteenth-century story reside the universal forces that drive the anxieties of human life. Gilman's supernatural fiction lends itself to existential interpretation because, while the ghosts and other supernatural phenomena are employed to enhance fear, they are also the thematic vehicles through which readers can explore their spirituality and sense of being. Grasping the impact of such literary analysis may be initially difficult for some students; however, small-group discussion and steadily progressive reading can help reluctant readers both find their own academic voices and form thoughtful relationships with Gilman's text. Exposing students to their own potential as readers catalyzes thoughtful classroom discussion and leads students to reflect independently upon the literature and its implications. Eleanor Kutz and Hephzibah Roskelly remind us in *An Unquiet Pedagogy*, "the reticence and disengagement of many high school and beginning college students arise from the fact that the readings seem so external to them" (217). Relinquishing the divide between the student and the text has to be a key factor in any classroom discussion. After all, and as Henry James writes, "As people feel life, so they will feel the art that is most closely related to it" (16). Hence, teachers of "The Yellow Wall-paper" should stress to their students, following Eleanor Kutz and Hephzibah Roskelly's guidance, "Not only must readers be active and work hard at constructing meanings, but they must also make choices, guess about possibilities, ask and answer questions as they proceed" (191). The function of any existential approach to "The Yellow Wall-paper" is therefore two-fold. First, the approach is designed to relate "The Yellow Wall-paper" to the actual society that surrounds our students' developing lives. Second, the approach is meant to provide students with the opportunity to voice their opinions through constructive and analytical classroom debate about Gilman's narrator and existentialism.

Allowing students access to both Simone de Beauvoir's *Second Sex* and Søren Kierkegaard's *The Sickness unto Death* facilitates learning about how Gilman's text can be applied to our everyday lives and so elucidates how the text can be read less as an historical study and more as an everyday journal of human suffering and experience. Relating anxieties expressed in Gilman's fiction to these writings of existential philosophy, teachers can draw students away from superficial stereotyping and toward a more complex understanding of Gilman's narrator and her expectations in life.

The reader comes to know the narrator through her secretive journal entries. Such an intimate presentation initially warms the reader to the narrator; indeed, one seems to know and understand the torment of her situation. However, as literary critics Jeanette King and Pam Morris acknowledge, this strategy both manipulates the reader's emotions and conceals textual facts. They suggest, therefore, that the curious reader should "look for the heroine *behind* the text" instead of necessarily for the one portrayed though the words of the text (28). They identify that a conflict exists between the narrator's "two selves" and state that while the first unnamed self enjoys the comforts of marriage, the second self challenges both society and traditional spirituality. Here they address a key issue within Gilman studies because they clearly note this second self is named Jane and that Jane names herself at the close of the text. They also emphasize when this second self explicitly names herself as "Jane," she is emphasizing the difference between her role as the passive wife of John and the heroine who has "got out at last" (28–29). King and Morris recognize that the battle between the two selves allows Jane to gain courage and a stronger sense of identity (28). The existential writings of Simone de Beauvoir and Søren Kierkegaard provide important insights into both halves of this complex heroine and hence also illuminate Gilman's text in different, yet equally productive, ways.

Literary character analysis is, by its very nature, complex and hence a rigorous structure is necessary to explore the various facets of any individual character's nature. The instructor should stress to the students that the first section of the project shall be dedicated to reading Beauvoir's *The Second Sex* alongside "The Yellow Wall-paper" and to exploring the existential struggle of Jane, a female trapped within a male-dominated world. The instructor should then stress that the second section of the project will build on such understandings through careful analysis of Jane's despair via Søren Kierkegaard's *The Sickness unto Death*. The first section shall study Jane's actions as an ordinary woman rebelling against the restrictions of a patriarchal society; the second section shall study Jane's extra-ordinary ability to use her female power to overpower John, her specific male oppressor. Together, the two sections shall parallel Jane's evolution from a trapped female to that of a liberated, and yet tormented, individual.

As an instructor at a four-year institution, I have found integrating Beauvoir and Kierkegaard into my survey of American literature classes very productive because I believe students of upper- as well as lower-level classes find existential theory aids their understanding of literature and its context in their lives. Throughout my classes I have found creating a coherent and steadily progressive program for reading both of these existential theorists is very important for the students. To facilitate steady learning, both sections are hence designed to illuminate central themes related to Gilman's text and to correlate with elements of the students' own lives. The themes are arranged to enhance students' understanding of Jane's gradual movement toward madness. The students can thus chronologically research and comprehend Jane's evolution through the following allotted course sections:

Section	**Author**	**Text**	**Topic for Discussion**
Section One	Simone de Beauvoir	*The Second Sex*	Jane's Character Jane's Home Jane's Drama
Section Two	Søren Kierkegaard	*The Sickness unto Death*	Jane's Struggle Jane's Despair Jane's Second Self
Closure	Beauvoir/ Kierkegaard		Jane's Final Emancipation

Each section can last as long as the instructor deems necessary but should be accompanied by class time divided among a) classroom discussion, b) small-group activities, c) personal journal entries. The instructor should stress this structure is designed to allow readers to comprehend how Jane's actions reflect Beauvoir's insights and yet also rebel against what Kierkegaard considers humanity's limitations. Hence, the instructor should emphasize that, while the section on Beauvoir will emphasize Jane's similarity to other women, the section on Kierkegaard will emphasize how Jane's unique position gives her a particular form of existential empowerment.

Existential Theorists

BEAUVOIR: In *The Second Sex*, Simone de Beauvoir applies existential theory and intuition to the female situation and so develops significant understandings of the relationships between women and men. Beauvoir observes, "the tragedy of marriage is not that it fails to assure woman promised happiness—but that it mutilates her; it dooms her to repetition and routine" (451). She also starkly insists that the "symbolic behavior through which women seek escape can lead to mental decay, obsessions, even crimes" (449). Beauvoir's work gains a powerful relevance as students become better aware of both the sexual stereotypes that continue to pervade society and the many thousands of "silenced" women who potentially share Jane's identity.

Beauvoir argues that female dejection and mental degeneration are created out of a male tradition of patriarchy. She believes that women's lives are ruined by idiosyncratic labeling and hopeless power struggles: "to say that a woman is a mystery is to say, not that she is silent, but that her language is not understood; she is there, but hidden behind veils" (241). She adds that "woman has a doubled and deceptive visage: she is all that man desires and all that he does not attain" (184). To further her argument, she examines various female situations and explores the constructions that society uses to define women. She says that the male/female issue is too often contested according to "fallacious" dichotomies. Noting Aristotle's contention that "we should regard the female nature as afflicted with a natural defectiveness," she writes angrily that "we must get out of [such] ruts," and "we must discard vague notions of superiority, inferiority, equality which have hitherto corrupted every discussion of the subject" (xvi). The crux of her argument is that we "must start afresh" with our perceptions of women and our existence (xxvi).

KIERKEGAARD: Søren Kierkegaard, wrestling with the concepts of religion, death, and humanity's relationship with eternity, elucidates in his writing many of the anxieties that troubled the first half of the nineteenth century. Kierkegaard highlights the various limitations he feels humanity imposes on itself. He suggests that humanity has meaning beyond its temporal existence and that humanity is morally responsible for the consequences of its own condition. Much of Kierkegaard's work captures the essence of humanity's terrible and often illusionary relationship with the unknown. Allowing the student-reader to become aware of both the power of self-re-evaluation and of re-reading Jane's terrible predicament enables a class to address key issues surrounding humanity's continuingly troubled and complex existence.

Kierkegaard's *The Sickness unto Death* specifically exposes students to the paradoxical nature of humanity through the study of the different "selves," finite and infinite, temporal and eternal, of a human being. In *The Sickness unto Death*, Kierkegaard examines the angst that one suffers as one prepares, through life, for the termination and silence of death. Deliberately provocative, this work relates that humanity's despair of life and this universe is born out of fear of life and of death. Application of *The Sickness unto Death* captures the torment of Jane as she battles against the restrictions of both her mind and society. Jane's form of depression makes life difficult for her. Indeed, at one point she clearly acknowledges, "Nobody would believe what an effort it is to do what little I am able—to dress and entertain, and order things" (31). She also admits "I cry at nothing, and cry most of the time" (34). She wishes she could escape her present life, but, until she starts to listen to the ghosts and hauntings of her imagination, such a transition is closed to her. Consequently, employing Kierkegaard in relation to the writings of Gilman and Beauvoir allows students to explore the existential repercussions of his or her own angst alongside Jane's terrible torment and subsequent "escape."

Incorporating Beauvoir

Jane's Character

THEORY: Jane believes that she is a "mere ordinary" person who feels both bound and silenced by the restrictions of her Victorian society (29). Her main tormentor is her husband, John. He is not an obviously evil man, but his patriarchal outlook on life makes him incompatible with Jane and her struggle for freedom and self-expression. The text notes that John "is very careful and loving" but that he "hardly lets [Jane] stir without special direction" (30). Jane explains she is suffering from "nervous troubles" and from a "slight hysterical tendency" (29). Jane suffers anxiety because her husband dictates her every action and so erases her identity. Significantly though, this presentation of the Victorian male/female relationship is not necessarily fiction.

Beauvoir clearly states, "throughout history women have always been subordinated to men" (xxi). She explains that the fundamental drama of the female is that she is forced to live in a world where men "compel her to assume the status of the Other" and where "they stabilize her as an object and so doom her to immanence" (xxviii). Beauvoir adds, "the term 'female' imprisons woman in her sex" (xxviii). She points out, however, that "the young wife very seldom admits her feelings to herself" and so, instead, "persists in her pretense of love through morality, hypocrisy, pride, or timidity" (436). Sometimes, however, "she submits with masochistic pleasure: she assumes the role of victim and her resignation is only a long, silent reproach; but it may often happen also that she engages in open battles with her master and often insists on tyrannizing over him in return" (439).

Like the women Beauvoir describes, Jane initially plays the role of the submissive young wife. However, the longer she and John stay in their "ghostly" old mansion, the more she finds herself turning first to reproach and then—as her mind turns itself increasingly inward—to anger (30). The story centers on this transformation, as Jane reduces her husband's mastery over her and rejects her status as Other. The movement yields many victories for Jane, but the new situation demands that she relinquish both her relationship with John and many stereotypical roles of her female sexuality. Consequently, the complexity of this bittersweet text allows the student both to celebrate Jane's existential empowerment and to pity her imprisoned and ghostly state.

APPLICATION: Referring to Jane's trapped state and Beauvoir's writing, the instructor should create a classroom dialogue that explores the perceived balance between male and female power within American society. The instructor should clearly emphasize to the students that traditionally upper-class white males reside within the center of American life while females, and thus also Jane, have resided and may still yet reside within the associated margins. To illustrate this dichotomy, the instructor should draw a circle on the board and write, according to student opinion, the various characteristics that have led men to succeed throughout American history. The instructor should then call the contents of this circle the "center" and identify all else as "Other." Outside the circle the instructor should write the characteristics students believe have prevented women from succeeding. Students will most likely and predictably characterize the "center" with such words as strength, wealth, independence and the "Other" with such words as motherhood, passivity, and dependence. Teachers should then request that students quietly determine their own places within this scenario as well as recognize that Jane's position as "Other" depreciates her worth to those in the "center." Language privileges men, separating them from women; however, as language engenders humanity, so, too, can it empower those who strive to be free. Hence, students should be encouraged to realize that, while Jane-as-Other cannot enter the circle, she can existentially empower herself by manipulating her femininity in ways that males do not expect.

Jane's Home

THEORY: Jane describes her home as "the most beautiful place" but admits that there is "something strange" about its presence (30). Beauvoir remarks that the family home can have a significant impact upon the psychology of both men and women: "Today the house has lost its patriarchal splendor; for the majority of men it is only a place to live, no longer freighted with the memory of dead generations, no longer encompassing the generations to come. But still the woman is all for giving her 'interior' the meaning and value that the true house and home once had" (423). Jane, like so many other women, still feels the weight of "dead generations." She is also carefully attuned to the potential history of the room and so explains, "There are things in that paper that nobody knows but me, or ever will" (35). She sympathizes with the "gouged" floor and the bed that looks like its been through the "wars," but she has no way to express the associated pain until she becomes a part of its cruel cycle herself (33). As a way to strengthen her own feminine identity, Jane aligns herself with the "dead generations" whose dirt is engrained within the wallpaper and whose memories and ghosts haunt the playroom.

Beauvoir notes that "homes" can become "haunted by the impalpable femininity" of female tenants (167). She points out that a woman can haunt a house with her presence; she can become "the soul" of a house, of the family, of the home (165). Gilman's story takes these observations to dramatic and ironic lengths. The "foulness" of the yellow wallpaper "creeps all over the house," and so Jane "find[s] it hovering in the dining-hall, skulking in the parlor, hiding in the hall, lying in wait for [her] on the stairs" (38). In such hallucinations, Jane is not alone. Beauvoir notes, "a household, with its meticulous and limitless tasks, permits to woman a sadomasochistic flight from herself in a state of distraction and mental vacancy" (426). As part of this "flight" is derived from the pain of being "confined within the conjugal sphere" that is the home, a woman has no choice but to "to change her prison into a realm" (424). To explore this notion, Beauvoir refers to Gaston Bachelard, who writes that a woman, confined to her home, will often make out of her world "a kind of counter-universe or universe in opposition" (424). This assertion captures Jane's movement, as she strives to create a world and a persona that is other to those of her everyday life.

Jane's perverted creations grow from her desolate condition, and so loneliness seems delicious to her. She comes to enjoy the wallpaper, but then she also recalls she "used to lie awake as a child and get more entertainment and terror out of blank walls and plain furniture than most children could find in a toy store" (32). This passage implies that, throughout her life, Jane has been able to read her surroundings as clearly as we read the text. Consequently, within the wallpaper she explains she can see "a strange, provoking, formless sort of figure, that seems to skulk about behind [the yellow wallpaper]" (33) and that the wallpaper "looks to [her] as if it *knew* what a vicious influence it had!" (32). Significantly, Beauvoir admits in her autobiographical text "The Prime of Life" that "to have a door that I could shut [out the rest of the world with] was the height of bliss to me" and that she used to "bitterly hug" her "loneliness" (54–55).

APPLICATION: The instructor should engage students in a discussion of Jane's terrible situation and Beauvoir's autobiographical insights to allow them to explore their own experiences of loneliness and desolation. To foster such an exploration, the instructor should ask students to compile lists of emotions they associate with certain rooms in their homes. Then the instructor should ask them to choose a room of particular significance and to explore how they feel about individual pieces of furniture and about the composition of the room. The goal is to guide them to the realization that they "read" their personal landscapes as closely as does Jane and that they as are "entertained" by their room's décor and furnishings.

Coupling such an exploration with a discussion of how students "shut out" the world and manipulate loneliness through clever use of furniture, television, and music can lead students to realize that, similar to Jane and Beauvoir, we often use our imagination to block out the pain of isolation. Subsequently, as homework, students should be asked to document in their journals how they arrange the contents of their dormitory rooms to create feelings of independence, security, and pleasure. My results show that, as students realize their dependence upon material comforts, they empathize more carefully with Jane and her need for internal security.

Jane's Drama

THEORY: Beauvoir notes "masochistic behavior appears in the wife who seeks to arouse in her husband the master, the tyrant, that he is not in reality" (421). Beauvoir also recognizes, however, the danger in such reversals: "marriage gives rise to fantastic comedies and playacting between partners, which may threaten to destroy the boundary between appearance and reality" (421). Jane's masochistic tendencies initially define her husband as a tyrant; however, as Jane gains power, John's status is reduced to that of a "young man" (42). Such tendencies strengthen Jane as she reverses the dominant male/submissive female structure that had so contained her. The wallpaper creates this strength for her because its fantastical "possibilities," its haunted women, and its madness are far removed from the reality of the distant husband. Jane uses this power to mock the severity of her husband's narrow-minded attitudes, writing in her journal that John "seems very queer sometimes" (37) and that she doesn't "like the look in his eyes" (40). She stops "trusting" him, explaining that she can see through his pretence of kindness (40). She savors the freedom that creeping about the house at night brings and so records, "I'm feeling ever so much better! I don't sleep much at night, for it is so interesting to watch developments" (38). The pride that she develops strengthens her, allowing her to believe she has become superior to John. Indeed, she believes is now "angry enough to do something desperate" (41). Given Beauvoir's insights, such angry pride is obviously dangerous because Jane has blurred her "boundary between appearance and reality." Furthermore, that the source of the danger is Jane's movement toward liberation is especially important because so many students, especially young women in today's society, will work toward their own levels of future liberation.

APPLICATION: The language of Jane's journal chronicles her changing attitudes toward her husband. A person's sense of existential identity can be transformed by how other people utilize language to define and describe them. Hence, the instructor should encourage students to question, "How can language create and enclose people within selective, and often cruel, terminology?" In small-group discussions, the instructor should then facilitate discussions exploring how name-calling through formative childhood years, through high school experiences, and through subsequent family life can alter a person's perception of him or herself. Specifically, students should address how power struggles between men and women often result in damaging stereotypical labels. A man can reduce his wife, and *vice versa*, by the labels he applies to her status. The instructor should therefore also ask students, "How can people employ language to empower themselves within marriage?" A complementary exploration should then be made of the idea that such labels as "cleaners" and "child minders" weaken the social status of women while labels such as "protectors" and "money-makers" empower men. Directly addressing the understanding that the drama of contemporary society is maintained according to carefully crafted stereotypes will emphasize that males and females are essentially reduced and separated according to the lowest common denominators within society.

Incorporating Kierkegaard

Jane's Struggle

THEORY: Initially, Jane accepts that John "laughs" at her because she expects such ridicule within marriage (29). At the tale's opening, she wishes her husband did not control her life but can only passively question, "What can one do?" (29). At this stage, as a veritable slave to her husband, Jane binds herself to her master and so creates her own despair. Kierkegaard writes that women lose *themselves* because they are so devoted to men (183). Beauvoir's text similarly decrees, "if woman seems to be the inessential which never becomes the essential, it is because she herself fails to bring about this change" (xviii). In her despair, Jane suffers many of the tensions described by Kierkegaard and Beauvoir. Throughout the action, Jane both luxuriates in the distance she creates between her husband and her inner self and acknowledges the pain of being separated from her role in a successful marriage. Kierkegaard captures the essence of this contrary pull when he writes, "the self is a synthesis in which the finite is the limiting factor, and the infinite the expanding factor" (163). Jane feels the finite constructions of the gardens and of the nursery wall jar against the infinite beyond of the wallpaper and the country road. She feels "the despair of responsibility" of loving her husband, but she also feels the pull of her imagination and the freedom of her soul (164). Hence, as she draws away from her female role and into the world of the yellow wallpaper, her female struggle for independence becomes more that of any individual struggling for freedom in existence. Given this transition, this process of empowerment, reading Kierkegaard becomes fascinating as one learns of the terrible humanity of Jane's situation. Therefore, the focus of the students' study should now move away from Beauvoir, who is concerned with ordinary female struggles and toward Kierkegaard, who is concerned with ordinary human struggles.

The twist, though, is that none of Jane's later struggles is entirely ordinary. Therefore, Jane's later extraordinary behavior becomes especially remarkable because her determination goes beyond that which Kierkegaard deems capable of humanity. Jane uses the yellow wallpaper to reduce the distance between her needy soul and her desperate imagination. The yellow wallpaper serves many functions, but primarily it gives Jane a domain beyond that of her husband. The wallpaper sections off a part of the world where Jane can use her imagination to feel as though her needs are being met. In Kierkegaardian terms, "imagination is the reflection of the process of infinitizing the intensity of [such] mediums" as pain and loneliness (164). The consequence, however, is that through Jane's journey she takes herself so far into the realm of imagination and forgetfulness she loses her way back. Kierkegaard notes, "generally the fantastical is that which so carries a [person] out into the infinite that it carries him away from himself and therewith prevents him from returning to himself" (164). The wallpaper, for Jane, marks that point of no return. Once she has passed beyond its boundaries, she can return neither to her original existence nor to her husband.

Kierkegaard remarks, at this stage of despair "possibility appears to the self ever greater and greater, more and more things become possible, because nothing becomes actual. At last it is as if everything were possible—but this is precisely when the abyss has swallowed up the self" (169). He also notes that at this point it is not "reality" that the subject lacks but "necessity" (169). Jane has no need to stay in the "real" world—she disagrees with her husband's views as a doctor, and she dislikes her atrocious lifestyle as a wife (29). She also has no necessity to limit herself to the world of reality (32). Instead, she discovers that the fantastic worlds of possibility allow her the freedom to express herself as a being distinct from John.

APPLICATION: The instructor should question, "What 'powers' bind humanity within contemporary America?" and so allow students to realize humanity is carefully bound to such institutions as education, government, society, and the family. The instructor can then enquire, "How do we feel about the 'pull' of these 'powers'?" And so guide students to understand how homework, taxation, laws, and family ties restrict our daily lives. Each of these questions should open the classroom to further discussion and should expose students to the understanding that, like Jane, we are bound by forces initially outside our control.

To help students understand this concept, teachers might solicit opinions about how contemporary Americans view women. The class should be divided into subsections that each represent specific groups of stereotyped males: brothers, fathers, husbands, doctors, lawyers, construction workers, military officials, etc. Assuming their particular persona, each group could then create a short presentation that encapsulates their various perspectives of women and their roles in society. This task will emphasize that many American social groups still depreciate and subordinate the worth of women within society.

Subsequently, exploring the question, "Do women enjoy such subordination?" advocates study of Beauvoir and Kierkegaards' more complex assumptions. Students should document in their journals how they perceive the women they know to be depreciated by American society. Here students can investigate women's private roles within the family and public roles within society while reflecting upon any patriarchy's need to keep women maintained in certain clearly defined and non-threatening positions. In this regard, the activity will help students to see that Jane's transformations signal both her existential fear that her life is worthless and her ability to revolt against humanity's complex expectations.

Jane's Despair

THEORY: Throughout Jane's revolt, her "nervous troubles are dreadfully depressing" (31). Such depression is a clear consequence of her ability to envision her potential freedom as a crawling woman and yet also to feel the restrictions of being a housebound female. Although Jane's visions are particular to her, her symptoms of depression are not unique. In *The Sickness unto Death*, Kierkegaard, under the pseudonym of Anti-Climacus, explores the notion that despair is the sickness that plagues and destroys all of humanity. The root of this illness, this "sickness," is humanity's unstable state of being. Kierkegaard writes that humanity "is a synthesis of the infinite and the finite, of the temporal and the eternal, of freedom and necessity. A synthesis is a relation between two factors. So regarded [a person] is not yet a self" (146). Hence, a person, as an incomplete being, contrasts the temporality of the physical world, with its aging processes and its diseases, to the splendid infinitude of the universe, and feels torn between the reality of the finite human body and the infinite possibilities of the human soul.

Kierkegaard relates that our confinement, on this planet and in life, creates a despair that can destroy us. The significance is that Jane can be seen, in later stages of the tale, to be stronger than the despairing individuals Kierkegaard portrays in his work. Jane manipulates her despair, endures the different stages of its agony, and transfers herself from a submissive to dominant position. Significantly, she does not evade the pain of her despair but instead employs it to her advantage. She uses her developing strength to go beyond boundaries that Kierkegaard considers insurmountable. She allows herself to be both challenged by human fears and driven by supernatural forces toward freedom and into the yellow wallpaper.

Manipulating her understanding of the world, Jane focuses her energy on herself and relinquishes her love of John and their child. There is danger inherent in such self-determination though, for as Kierkegaard acknowledges, "the clearer the self-consciousness a man has in committing suicide, the more intense is his despair" (182). The existential despair that Jane suffers as she moves toward her mental suicide is intense, yet, contrary to Kierkegaard's perception, the resulting pain strengthens, not weakens, her. She feels herself "flourishing" as her body gets "better" (38). She allows her inner defiant self to use the despair as a vehicle through which to grow more powerful. When the "awful pattern" of the wallpaper "laughs" at her, she works with "pure spite" to tear off its outer layer and so actively relinquishes the role of passive observer (40–41).

APPLICATION: Scrutinizing such existential despair, students can become readily aware of the potential complexities inherent in literature and life. Hence, the instructor can emphasize to students Jane represents the struggle between self and spirit that troubles each one of us below the surface of our everyday lives. Life deposits us within our bodies and determines that we shall live out our lives without telling us why. It offers contradictions without resolution, and it determines that we shall endure death's inevitable presence. Students rarely admit their fear of death in public; however, as Kierkegaard highlights, "there lives not one single man who after all is not to some extent in despair, in whose inmost parts there does not dwell a disquietude, a perturbation, a discord, an anxious dread of an unknown something [. . .] a sickness of the spirit" (155). The consequence is that students can realize in this "despair one often does not dare to believe in himself, finds it too venturesome a thing to be himself, far easier and safer to be like the others, to become an imitation, a number, a cipher in the crowd" (166).

To create a small-group activity focused on the anonymity of humanity's fears within contemporary society yields interesting and productive results. Students adapt to a variety of social molds without necessarily realizing they often do so because they fear the venture of "standing out." To heighten the students' awareness of their own perhaps-unspoken fears, the instructor should ask students anonymously to write their own anxieties onto blank cards. After a short period of time, these cards should be distributed randomly among the students. Dialogue can then be created from such questions as "What do we, as a class, most seem to 'anxiously dread' in our daily lives?" and "Given such anxieties, do you believe humanity is justified in its fears and disquietudes?" The resulting discussion, reflecting both upon Kierkegaard and the students' own perceptions of life, will enable students to discuss more deeply Jane's despair as a human, not fictional, condition.

Furthermore, a cohesive pedagogical approach to analyzing the catalysts of Jane's despair can be created from three separate tasks. First, the instructor should request that students study the society during Jane's era and specifically the use of mental institutions for women. Inviting students to use history will help them to understand Jane's desperate and limited options. Second, the instructor should divide students into those in favor of and those against Jane's transformation and create a forum that allows students to voice whether or not they are sympathetic to Jane's existential situation. Third, the instructor should assign for journal work the question, "How do our personalities evolve throughout our lives?" and therefore require students both to theorize existentially about their own complex lives and to recognize that, similar to Jane, human personalities adapt to survive change and trauma.

Jane's Second Self

THEORY: As Jane revolts and becomes "angry enough to do something desperate," she "cultivates deceit," relinquishes her passivity, and actively searches for the "role" which will allow her to redefine her relationship with John. Kierkegaard writes that the darkest level of despair comes when one "wishes for a new [replacement] self" (186). Curiously, however, Kierkegaard also calls this level "ludicrous" and so implies the impossibility of both his subject's and Jane's desire. Thus Jane's second self achieves what Kierkegaard intimates is impossible. He writes that "there can be no question" that one self cannot slip away from another (196). However, and to use Kierkegaard's language, her created second self "hates its [first] self" so severely that it is able to shift away and become separate (196). Kierkegaard also maintains that humanity cannot go beyond despair, that we forever trap ourselves within its dialectics; however, Jane moves through such stages and so transforms herself into a being that at least appears to be without despair (185). Kierkegaard emphasizes that each individual is a weak, "passive suffering" self (194). In contrast, Gilman's female figure is invigorated as she moves beyond the limitations of her place and through the dimensions of her imagination. Kierkegaard's men find their "dwelling places distasteful," but "they do not move out," and they do not change. Instead, they "swing away entirely from the inward direction which is the path they should have followed in order to become truly selves" (189). In contrast, Gilman's character engages with herself fully; she speaks to her inner beings and so embarks with commitment on the "inward direction" that leads to her new form of being. She, unlike many of the men in Kierkegaard's society, has "learned to fear," and she has brought herself to travel through the "disconsolate desert" in which so many men rest (190–191).

APPLICATION: Emphasizing the differences between the first and second selves allows students to recognize the depths of Jane's internal divide. The instructor should assign one half of the class to categorize characteristics (e.g., domesticity, fear, humility) of the first Jane and then the other half of the class to categorize characteristics of the second Jane (e.g., independence, courage, pride). This movement will highlight Jane's commitment to change. However, students should then be drawn to recognize that as the second Jane emerges, the weaker Jane is left behind and that perhaps they would not be capable of such a final division. The instructor should ask the class to record within their journals departures that they themselves have recently made and so allow them to quietly reflect upon the pain of leaving loved ones and comfortable, if not perfect, situations.

The instructor should coax the students to discuss in small groups their life's ambitions and to identify the various ways they have not been able to manifest their individual dreams. The instructor should ask students to reflect, in journal entries, upon what events altered their ambitions. Initially such concerns as money and location will be analyzed, but then, as students investigate further, emotions such as fear, pride, and insecurity should emerge as the more existential reasons why the various paths of their development changed course. One hopes that many students shall then begin to admire, and even envy, Jane's journey toward her truer-more-honest form of being.

Jane's Final Emancipation

THEORY: As the tale nears closure, the narrator becomes possessive: "I am here, and no person touches this paper but me—not *alive*!," and in that possessive state she externally vocalizes her anger, something the meeker Jane would never have done (41). Furthermore, at the moment when the narrator gains her name, Jane, the text gains a new voice, and that new voice embodies a self that is different from Jane-the-victim: "'I've got out at last' said I, 'in spite of you and Jane! And I've pulled off most of the paper, so you can't put me back!'" (42).

As a reader, one probably has to accept that this statement means that Jane's inner self has detached itself from its body and has placed itself within the wallpaper. The liberated second self takes pleasure in its freedom, but grief shapes the supposed joy of Jane's reality. The second self gains power, but in the shift the created other is silenced. The power of this second being is that it has altered its contract with existence—it has little to do with humanity's expectations and has, as its created playground, a land beyond the reach of the "sane" or "sensible." It enters a world that is, as it rejects the expected world, more distinctly *unto death*. Kierkegaard explains that through "self-duplication," the "self labors itself into the direct opposite, [and so] it becomes really no self" (202). Similarly, Gilman's female speaker lets go of her hold on the excruciatingly controlled temporal world so that she can explore the wilderness that is the eternal terrain of the madwoman. She refutes her husband's right to dictate her life, and she emancipates herself to explore worlds beyond the chains of reality. She allows the possibilities and violence of her new self to dictate her being and so endures the journey away from controlling and restricting selves.

APPLICATION: Students should recognize that our distance from Jane at the closure of "The Yellow Wall-paper" is painful. As readers, students and teachers alike are left behind at the end of the tale with the powerless husband; as readers, not one of us can "put [Jane] back" (42). The instructor should address that sense of loss and confusion because it is of central importance to meaning of the text. However, the instructor should also emphasize the understanding that, unlike the husband, students' have clear minds to read Jane's diary, classroom time, and now their existential insights to establish thoughtful discussions on the existential evolution of Jane's madness and the creation of her new being.

Once such a perspective has been established, the instructor should ask each of the students to assume the persona of John and to write a short essay or monologue that captures his sense of isolation and incomprehension. Once each short piece has been written, the instructor should collect them all and then redistribute them randomly so that each student gains control of someone else's work. The instructor should then require students to assume the persona of either Beauvoir or Kierkegaard and to reconsider carefully the perspectives each offers of humanity's insecurity in the face of isolation. From that position, the students should then be required to critique the fears that "John" explores through "his" essay. Once this second task has been completed, all essays should be returned to their original owners so that each student can return home and reflect in his or her journal on the existential readings, on John and Jane's private evolutions, and on how the ending of "The Yellow Wall-paper" affected him or her as a student and as an intelligent reader.

Repercussions

The repercussions of any reader's relationship with Jane are as curious as they are manifold. One potential and terrible truth is that we envy Jane in the moment that we admire her. Beauvoir sees this contradiction in human life, and so writes that, while we love one another, "it is unacceptable, inconceivable that one should be free if the others are not" (*Adieux* 359). The strain of the narrator's relationship with reality and with ourselves makes us humble. Jane has placed herself before the terror of her being, and she has faced the emptiness of her soul. Not all who read this text can say that they have ever had such courage. Kierkegaard says we have forgotten what it is to exist (Wahl 4). Exposing the pain of this proposition to a class of students, while reflecting upon the literature of Gilman, Beauvoir, and Kierkegaard, allows a teacher to reveal that the emptiness of humanity resides within *all* of us, not just within a figure of the nineteenth-century tortured female such as Jane.

Works Cited

Beauvoir, Simone de. *Adieux*. Trans. Patrick O'Brian. New York: Pantheon, 1984.

——. "The Prime of Life." *The Penguin Book of Women's Lives*. Ed. Phyllis Rose. London: Penguin, 1995: 53–68.

——. *The Second Sex*. Trans. H.M. Parshley. New York: Bantam, 1961.

Dock, Julie Bates, Comp. and Ed. *Charlotte Perkins Gilman's "The Yellow Wall-paper" and the History of Its Publication and Reception: A Critical Edition and Documentary Casebook*. University Park, PA: The Pennsylvania State University Press, 1998.

Gilman, Charlotte Perkins. "The Yellow Wallpaper." 1892. *Charlotte Perkins Gilman's "The Yellow Wall-paper and the History of Its Publication and Reception: A Critical Edition and Documentary Casebook*. Comp. and Ed. Julie Bates Dock. University Park, PA: The Pennsylvania State University Press, 1998. 29–42.

James, Henry. *The Art of Fiction, and Other Essays*. New York: Oxford University Press, 1948.

Kierkegaard, Søren. *Fear and Trembling / The Sickness unto Death*. Trans. Walter Lowrie. New York: Doubleday, 1954.

King, Jeanette, and Pam Morris. "On Not Reading Between the Lines: Model of Reading in 'The Yellow Wallpaper.'" *Studies in Short Fiction* 26 (1989): 23–32.

Kutz, Eleanor, and Hephzibah Roskelly. *An Unquiet Pedagogy: Transforming Practice in the English Classroom*. Portsmouth: Boynton, 1991.

Wahl, Jean. *Philosophies of Existence*. Trans. F. M. Lory. New York: Schocken, 1969.

Jim O'Loughlin

TEACHING GENRE THROUGH "THE YELLOW WALL-PAPER"

Any text can be taught by emphasizing genre, though it is a challenging concept to use well. Charlotte Perkins Gilman's "The Yellow Wall-paper" offers unique pedagogical opportunities because of the history of its relationship to specific genres of writing. But making the most of those opportunities requires a considered approach. If students are instructed to simply look for generic characteristics and then to pigeonhole texts, they will do little thoughtful analysis. However, if students think of genre as a way in which expectations are created for readers, then they can begin to interrogate their own reading practices.

The exercise outlined in this article is based upon literature classes I have taught on "The Yellow Wall-paper." In these classes, I present Gilman's text alongside Edgar Allan Poe's short story, "The Fall of the House of Usher," and the section of Gloria Steinam's *Outrageous Acts and Everyday Rebellions* about her mother's battles with mental illness entitled "Ruth's Song." The point of these pairings is for students to consider whether "The Yellow Wall-paper" is best classified generically as a gothic or a feminist story. This exercise intentionally parallels scholarly debate about Gilman's text and offers a ready introduction to critical issues surrounding the story. But, furthermore, the exercise allows students to experience first hand how generic expectations can shape readers' experiences and guide interpretations.

Reception as Context

When I first taught this section, I emphasized how gothic approaches to "The Yellow Wall-paper" had been superceded by feminist methodologies. Following critical thinking at the time, I felt I was mirroring an historical transformation in responses. Put forward most influentially by Elaine Hedges in her "Afterword" to the 1973 Feminist Press reissue of "The Yellow Wall-paper," this version of reception history claimed that early readers of the story saw it "essentially as a Poe-esque tale of chilling horror—and as a story of mental aberration" (39). It was only a more recent generation of readers that read the story from a feminist perspective, recovering it as a tale of the sexual politics of marriage and the psychological toll of patriarchal oppression.

This account of the text's reception drew primarily from Gilman's own writings about "The Yellow Wall-paper." It also inspired critics who viewed their work as part of a recovery of silenced feminist writers. However, that narrative of neglect-turned-appreciation has come under fire recently, most substantially by Julie Bates Dock. Dock's research into the story's reception history has revealed a different tale. Dock insists that Gilman's initial readers did not neglect the sexual politics of "The Yellow Wall-paper," pointing to a number of contemporaneous reviews that identified "the cause of the narrator's insanity as her husband" (19). Dock also puts into question Gilman's own account of the story's reception, noting, for example, that Gilman herself made connections between her story and the writings of Poe (87).

What also emerges from Dock's research on "The Yellow Wall-paper" is not that this story was neglected and in need of recovery but rather that it has been read continuously as part of different genres. Even a cursory glance at the story's republication record (which Dock provides), shows the variety of contexts within which "The Yellow Wall-paper" has been considered over the past century. For example, in 1942 "The Yellow Wall-paper" appeared in Philip Van Doren Stern's anthology, *The Midnight Reader: Great Stories of Haunting and Horror*; a year later it was published as part of Helene Reed's *About Women: A Collection of Short Stories*. In 1985 the story was reprinted in both *The Norton Anthology of Literature by Women* and a collection entitled *Haunted Women: The Best Supernatural Tales by American Women Writers*. More recently the *Penguin Putnam American Literature Anthology 2000* catalog includes "The Yellow Wall-paper" as part of *Four Stories by American Women* as well as in *American Gothic Tales, The Portable American Realism Reader*, and *The Signet Book of American Short Stories* (Penguin). Generically, feminism, the gothic, and even realism have served as categories through which to understand "The Yellow Wall-paper."

Dock uses her discoveries to discredit feminists' account of their own involvement in this story's reception history. And while that account surely needs revision, Dock's intramural squabbling has the effect of diminishing the most significant aspects of her own work. Feminist critics may not have rediscovered "The Yellow Wall-paper," but their approaches have always been an important part of this text's reception. Since its publication, the story has been read in a variety of generic contexts. The issue now is to figure out what difference these contexts have made in how the story is read and interpreted. In teaching "The Yellow Wall-paper," I aim to have students tackle these questions and to see how complex a simple question like, "What is 'The Yellow Wall-paper' about?" can be.

Genre and What It's Not

Genre is a concept best defined when left ambiguous. As Michael Denning notes, genre can be used to describe either subject matter or formal attributes. Attempts to establish rigid generic categories invariably fail, as texts inevitably transcend and ignore these restrictions. Eschewing classification, Denning suggests instead that genre be thought of as "an account of a culture's transformations" (75). For Denning, genres become "enactments of social conflicts and cleavages," so that shifts in genre have a social correspondence (77). It is only as social beings that individuals come to recognize and respond to generic conventions. Though Denning's approach focuses on writing rather than reading, his insistence on the social contexts for genre serves as a valuable starting point.

A helpful addendum to Denning's definition of genre is provided in the textbook, *Reading Texts*. In the account provided there, the editors provide students with a definition of genre that considers the role of both readers and writers. They define genre as a "term used loosely to mean the 'kind' or 'form' of literature [. . .] There are no fixed or absolute distinctions among genres. They are largely the product of reader assumption and expectation, and as such are useful conventions rather than real categories" (McCormick 285). This account of genre focuses on the role of readers in making generic determinations. It also acknowledges the contingency of genres themselves. Both these qualifications are important for students if they are to avoid the problem of pigeonholing. But it is important to insist, following Denning, that readers' assumptions and expectations are something different than individual taste. Genres are social creations, understandable by a reader only by virtue of that reader's participation in a particular social formation.

For the following exercise to be successful, it is essential to remember that genres are socially created. The goals of the exercise detailed here are not only to provide students with a richer reading experience of "The Yellow Wall-paper" but to give them insights into the social forces that have shaped them as readers. It is only as students begin to question the "naturalness" of their own reading practices that the possibilities of new ways of reading take shape.

Texts as Context

The focus of this exercise is "The Yellow Wall-paper," but that is not the first text that students read. Instead I assign half the class Edgar Allan Poe's "The Fall of the House of Usher" while the other half reads Steinam's "Ruth's Song." Meeting either in separate sessions or as two groups sharing the same room (the latter is a more difficult teaching task), these half-classes are set up to read "The Yellow Wall-paper" as part of different generic contexts with different expectations. When students do read "The Yellow Wall-paper," they read it alongside of and in conversation with very different texts.

I chose the Poe story for two reasons. First, among those who classify "The Yellow Wall-paper" as gothic, Poe is the author with whom Gilman is most often compared. "Usher" is the story of Poe's with the most surface similarities to Gilman's text. As in "The Yellow Wall-paper," Poe's story involves a symbolic connection between character and place. Both stories also trace characters' mental development and emotional instability. I have found it helpful for students to place the story's concerns within a larger historical context, introducing students to the romantic critique of Enlightenment rationality. Some critics would chaff at labeling "Usher" as gothic—arguing, as I. M. Walker does, that all supposed supernatural elements of the story have "a rational interpretation" (47). I find that many qualities of the story, from the Usher castle to the atmosphere of gloom to the developing sense of terror, place it in a familiar category for students along with works by writers ranging from Mary Shelley to Stephen King.

Some students are turned off by the formal prose of Poe's narrator, so I have found that a little guidance at the beginning can be helpful. In particular, it is important to have students focus on the narrator's first view of the Usher castle. The building is described as almost a rotting skull, with eye-like windows surrounded by decayed trees. The story's narrator notes that the Usher family has become so identified with their dwelling that "House of Usher [was] an appellation which seemed to include, in the minds of the peasantry who used it, both the family and the family mansion" (3). From the very beginning of the story, locale and character are interlinked symbolically.

Much of what is significant in "Usher" is to be found in description rather than plot, so we focus more on Poe's language than on what happens in the story. Of course, we discuss the mysteries of the plot—What happens to Madeline? What is her relationship to Roderick? Why would the house collapse?—and I encourage students to look for the answers to those questions in prior descriptions. However, inevitably students must also fill in gaps in the story. For instance, at what point is Roderick aware of what has happened to his sister? He clearly knows of her fate before the narrator does, but does he realize that as soon as he hears noise, or does he know about his sister all along?

Answering some of these questions requires students to delve into Roderick's character, to hypothesize about his relationship with his sister, and to analyze Poe's language for clues as to how the external circumstances of the story reflect the inner turmoil of Roderick Usher. If students are uncertain about how to proceed, I offer two competing explanations of Usher's behavior. In one, Roderick has been involved in an incestuous relationship with his sister and entombs her as a way of hiding his guilt. In the second, Roderick is a character with a masculinity crisis. In burying his sister, he is attempting to expunge the feminine side of himself. Students tend to find both interpretations a bit of a stretch, so an analysis of Poe's language becomes crucial. Sections that had seemed previously unimportant, such as the description of Roderick's physical features, take on a new importance when used to test out an interpretation. In either case, both interpretations emphasize non-rational behavior; the narrator's obliviousness to what is happening around him operates as a critique of facile empiricism. The question students are left with, and it's one that leads right into "The Yellow Wall-paper," is what limits are there to a philosophically rational view of the world? What's left out and what doesn't count?

Meanwhile the other half of the class reads "Ruth's Song (Because She Could Not Sing It)", a chapter from Gloria Steinam's 1983 essay collection, *Outrageous Acts and Everyday Rebellions*. Paired with "The Yellow Wall-paper," Steinam's essay on her mother, Ruth, helps make explicit much of the feminist subtext of Gilman's story. "Ruth's Song" details how, after marrying, Steinam's mother grew increasingly isolated and subsequently became mentally ill. Steinam insists upon expanding her scope beyond her mother's individual story, analyzing what happened to Ruth in terms of the social forces that contributed to her mother's problems. As an illustration of the feminist credo, "the personal is political," Steinam's connection between the individual and the social offers insights that are implicit (though not always obvious to student readers) in "The Yellow Wall-paper."

Steinam's essay begins not with her mother but with the story of her Uncle Ed, a promising engineer who left his family and remarried "beneath him," eventually becoming the town handyman. Within Steinam's family there was much speculation about Ed's transformation. Some saw the Great Depression as a cause; others blamed some individual mental defect; still others suspected politics or religious belief might explain Ed's decisions. Steinam notes that while her relatives had no difficulty finding social causes for Ed's alteration, no such explanations were applied to her mother. The transformations in Ruth's life were understood, even by Ruth herself, as personal in nature.

The Ruth that Steinam writes about in the essay is different from the Ruth she remembers growing up. In many ways, the function of the essay is to fill in the crude contours of her childhood image of her mother. Steinam comes to realize that there was much more to Ruth than she could see as a daughter growing up in difficult circumstances. More importantly, she sees that Ruth could have been a much different person had she been able to live up to her creative and emotional potentials.

As Steinam reconstructs it, Ruth was an intelligent and successful local journalist who gave up her career when she married Steinam's father. Following her husband from job to job, Ruth became the mother of two daughters and found herself increasingly isolated in rural locations. Before Steinam was born, Ruth had already had her first nervous breakdown. Others followed, along with a period in a sanatorium. After her parents divorced, Steinam was raised by Ruth but often found herself taking care of a mother who was afraid to go out of the house.

In one crucial section, the only significant excerpt in Ruth's own words, Ruth tells of a time when, feeling isolated and abandoned at a remote location, she decided to walk five miles to the nearest store with her two daughters and their dog. Along the way, a car struck and seriously injured their dog. Ruth vowed to make the next car stop to help them, but there was no next car on this rural road. The dog died in her arms. Ruth and the children returned home. Marking this scene as a turning point in her life, Ruth told her husband, "From now on, I'm going with you. I won't bother you. I'll just sit in the car. But I can't bear to be alone again" (513). This scene in particular, but Ruth's story as a whole, mirrors the internal torment of the woman isolated from human contact in "The Yellow Wall-paper." Steinam realizes that "The family must have watched this energetic, fun-loving, book-loving woman turn into someone who was afraid to be alone, who could not hang on to reality long enough to hold a job, and who could rarely concentrate enough to read a book" (507).

As with Gilman's protagonist, Ruth undergoes a transformation in which those around her provide little comfort and are at times the source of her problems. Throughout the essay, Steinam reminds readers that were Ruth a different person, particularly a man like her Uncle Ed, she would have been treated much differently. But Ruth had been "cared for but not helped for twenty years," because, Steinam acidly realizes, "[Ruth's] functioning was not necessary to the world" (508). Steinam's emphasis on the gendered restrictions placed on her mother provides the crucial analytic perspective that students can bring to "The Yellow Wall-paper."

Walking the Tightrope

Admittedly the next section of this exercise poses some risk. It requires students to be aware of and engaged with the reading as well as the responses of their peers. I intentionally place students with different generic expectations into conversation with one another. This creates some confusion, but it is a productive confusion aimed toward encouraging students to rethink the assumptions and strategies of their own reading.

Following sessions on either "The Fall of the House of Usher" or "Ruth's Song," the class as a whole reads "The Yellow Wall-paper" and comes together to discuss it. After both sections of the class have read "The Yellow Wall-paper," I ask them to write answers to a series of questions, the most important of which is "What qualities make 'The Yellow Wall-paper' like the first text you read?" This question focuses attention on connections between texts and places "The Yellow Wall-paper" in a generic context. Students who read Poe are asked to explain how the wallpaper in Gilman's text comes to take on characteristics of the narrator's state of mind. Students who read Steinam are asked to show the way in which the narrator's changing state of mind is a response to the way she is treated by her husband. All students also write their own initial response to "The Yellow Wall-paper" that goes beyond the plot to detail what they feel is the central point or significance of the story: "What is this story about?" I insist that students note particular passages or lines that helped them reach their conclusions.

When the class comes together, I first break the students down into a Poe group and a Steinam group to go over the responses they have written. Then, crossing my fingers, we move into a whole-class discussion. In kicking off the discussion, I have found that the most provocative question, in that it provides the most contradictory responses, is "What is the significance of the wallpaper in this story?" I begin here, rather than following the narrative of the text, first to see how students have conceptualized the story but also to get some sample responses that the rest of the class can consider.

If it works, things get confusing. Different responses and divergent focuses emerge. Students wonder if they have all read the same story. Many who were first exposed to Poe discover that they paid little attention to the role of the husband in "The Yellow Wall-paper." If anything, they tend to see him as generally well intentioned but ineffective. Many who read Steinam initially view the mental state of Gilman's protagonist as having a much more rational explanation than do those who read Poe. In discussion, I insist that students support their claims by noting particular passages that seemed crucial to interpreting the story. Not surprisingly, the two groups often focus on different moments.

One specific line usually provokes contrasting responses. At the beginning of the story, the protogonist states, "John is a physician, and *perhaps*—(I would not say it to a living soul, of course, but this is dead paper and a great relief to my mind)—*perhaps* that is one reason I do not get well faster" (Gilman 29). Is the protagonist to be trusted here? Read literally, the emphasis on the word "perhaps" suggests the protagonist's uncertainty about her beliefs. But why then italicize it twice? This overemphasis suggests there could be more to her criticism than is apparent at first. For many students, the point here is counterintuitive. How could John's being a doctor be the cause of her continued illness?

I have found that the subtlety of this argument is difficult for students, but those who have read the Steinam essay are more attuned to the sexual politics of the story. Eventually, someone sees that John's combined role as doctor/husband gives him a traditional authority that remains unquestioned despite the protagonist's ongoing uncertainty about the course of treatment prescribed for her. For students who have read the Poe story, this focus on the husband's actions often seems puzzling. To many of them, John appears as an ancillary figure; few even question John's account of his wife's medical condition. However, if pushed, some of the Poe readers can see how John could be considered a representative of Enlightenment rationality.

Poe readers tend to focus more on the mechanics of the protagonist's downfall. When I ask the question, "When do you begin to question the speaker's reliability?," these students are more likely to have a ready answer. They can chart the protagonist's growing obsession with the wallpaper, noting when interest turns to identification. These students invariably point to one crucial scene in which Gilman's narrator begins to speak less of the surface of the paper and instead notices a level behind the surface. "Behind that outside pattern the dim shapes get clearer every day" (35). But when asked why the narrator becomes unreliable at that particular moment, these students tend to be stumped.

I then ask students to look at the beginning of the scene, when the protagonist tells of a "real earnest reasonable talk" during which she attempted to get John to let her visit relatives and get out of the imposed rest cure for a while (35). John refuses, and the protagonist finds herself not up to the confrontation, breaking into tears as she tried to convince him otherwise. Attuned to the role of John at this point, students from throughout the class then can point to the protagonist's limited outlets for action and her husband's refusal to take her concerns seriously. Some Steinam readers may also recognize a thematic parallel with the scene in "Ruth's Song" in which Ruth is unable to do anything to help the pet dog that died in her arms. This scene in "The Yellow Wall-paper" serves as a similar breaking point.

The final interpretive chasm between these two groups of student readers comes at the end of the story. When asked to make sense of the narrator's breakdown, many of the Poe students find that the question doesn't make sense. The protagonist has gone insane; what sense could there be in that? I ask students to re-read the second-to-last paragraph in the story, when John has come into the locked room and found his wife disheveled and crawling along the sides of the room. "'I've got out at last,' said I, 'in spite of you and Jane! And I've pulled off most of the paper, so you can't put me back!'" (42). In my experience, many students caught up in the story's plot miss the importance of this line. But when asked to reconsider the above passage, I've had students note that this is the first time that the protagonist has identified herself with the woman behind the paper, and this identification forces some students to rethink their previous interpretation. At this point, I introduce the concept of projection and suggest a psychological explanation of what is happening in these concluding lines. I have had strong students make a connection between the protagonist's projection and her prior restricted scope of movement and activity. The question, and it is one that tends to divide down generic lines, is whether there is a method to the protagonist's madness.

I have also found that it is only with prodding that students will attempt to figure out the mystery of "Jane," the name mentioned for the first time in the above passage. Many readers (I was one of them my first time through) simply read Jane as "Jennie," the sister-in-law who has helped take care of the protagonist. Some students see the discrepancy but write it off as a misprint (as some editors of the story have according to Dock, who notes "corrections" of this line on 122–30). What I have to ask students to do is to read the line out of context, as if there was no story attached to it, and then say what they think it might mean. I have had students volunteer that Jane must be a woman with whom John was having an affair. The protagonist has said nothing about an affair directly, so some question this interpretation. Other students point to John's absences and the protagonist's annoyance at them. I leave this question up in the air, as a mystery to be debated rather than solved. As we conclude, I make sure to recap the discussion and ask students to write about how their response to the story compared with those of their peers. I have never videotaped one of these classes, but I can envision how a record of the discussion could prove to be a valuable resource.

In describing the exercise to this point, I have concentrated on how most students have responded or have suggested tendencies among groups of readers. But it has also been important for me as a teacher to recognize that responses do not necessarily correspond to the generic conventions provided for students. Genre has its limits; it provides only one of the variables governing students' readings. I have found that some, though by no means all, female students see the feminist subtext of "The Yellow Wall-paper" and are more sympathetic to the narrator, no matter which story they have read first. Additionally, when introduced to new ways of reading the story, some students immediately jump ship, so to speak, adapting an interpretive model better suited to their predispositions. But other students, in fact a majority, tend to stick with the way they first read the story, either as a gothic or a feminist text.

I have been surprised to see that this persistence remains despite the next part of the exercise. I next spill the beans, explaining the purpose of the exercise much as I have here, and going over the basic principles of genre. For the following class session, students read the essay that had been previously withheld from them—Steinam for the Poe students, Poe for the Steinam students—and we come together for a discussion of the three texts. I attempt not to repeat too much material in this class, even though one text is new for each student. Often I try to have one group of students teach the other, asking the initial Steinam group to explain key feminist terms or having the original Poe group describe gothic. I also have supplemented this discussion with a historical survey of the reception of "The Yellow Wall-paper."

For the paper assignment at the end of this section, I ask students not just to write about the texts but to focus on how their interpretation evolved over the course of the exercise. Students must answer whether they think "The Yellow Wall-paper" is best classified as gothic or feminist. I insist that students must choose one of these categories, recognizing that arguments can be made in support of both. There is a danger that students will attempt to take the easy way out and not make a decision, feeling that since either choice could be made that neither is correct. By asking students to show how they came to reach a decision, the assignment emphasizes the work they do as readers and how genre works on them.

In these papers, I look for students to consider genre in terms of social conventions and to consider their participation in those conventions. In the end, the exercise should not be about justifying personal preferences but coming to understand the way in which what seems personal can be socially determined. At the same time, students should measure the limits of social determination to figure out both the force and the limitations of generic expectations. Some students find that key passages from the text were important to their interpretations. Others say that classroom discussions helped them make up their minds. Still others rely on their prior readerly predispositions (Stephen King fans always insist that gothic is the best choice). I ask students to weigh all these options, though understandably some loom larger than others. The narrative of their responses ideally should draw on informal writing they have done up to this point. The best of the papers I have received have been able to chart a narrative of development in which interpretations are tested and then either confirmed or found wanting. Many students make good use of classroom discussions. I am always surprised to find out that the quiet student I thought was not paying attention was in fact listening closely and reconsidering her or his thoughts on the text.

The assignment also demands that students confront a variety of critical questions. Students both hostile to and supportive of feminism must think about how they came by their beliefs and how those beliefs affected their reading. Some students struggle to understand why certain ways of reading make sense for some people but not others. When required to make a choice between two defensible options, students work as critical thinkers, coming to appreciate the necessity of interpretation as well as the ways in which interpretations can be conditioned by genre.

In Retrospect

It can be difficult as a teacher to suspend critical judgment, even temporarily. Our training does not encourage us to put forward different interpretative possibilities and then fail to choose between them. Like most academic readers of "The Yellow Wall-paper" (though perhaps not most general readers), I am persuaded by many aspects of the feminist interpretation of this text, and I'm sure that that was clear in my presentation of this exercise. In fact, it was easier to teach "The Yellow Wall-paper" before the publication of Julie Bates Dock's work, when the reigning critical narrative involved a feminist approach "correcting" the gothic one. But I think it is actually more valuable to students when there are unanswered questions surrounding "The Yellow Wall-paper."

Though I believe "The Yellow Wall-paper" is an exemplary text for studying the role of genre, this exercise could be performed on any number of texts with intriguing generic origins. Readers never approach a text without some expectations, but those expectations are not usually acknowledged. Making the role of genre explicit makes students aware of the complexity of the work they do as readers. The crucial thing I have learned from this experience is to present the texts involved and the critical questions to be answered as truly up for debate. In essence, this approach follows Gerald Graff's call to "teach the conflicts" (see Graff, particularly Chapter 3). Rather than letting the issue of feminist vs. gothic classifications be something an instructor irons out before a lecture, critical conflict becomes the basis of inquiry. In some of the most intriguing student papers from this exercise, students have been initially baffled as to how the person sitting next to them could "be so wrong" but have gone on to consider the specific social influences on their own reading. The power of genre as a teaching tool lies not in classifying texts but in highlighting the social formations underlying all reading and writing. In the case of "The Yellow Wall-paper," a literary investigation into the text soon opens out onto cultural questions surrounding composition and reception.

Works Cited

Denning, Michael. *Mechanic Accents: Dime Novels and Working-Class Culture in America.* New York: Verso, 1987.

Dock, Julie Bates, Comp. and Ed. *Charlotte Perkins Gilman's "The Yellow Wall-paper" and the History of Its Publication and Reception: A Critical Edition and Documentary Casebook.* University Park, PA: The Pennsylvania State University Press, 1998.

Gilman, Charlotte Perkins. "The Yellow Wallpaper." 1892. *Charlotte Perkins Gilman's "The Yellow Wall-paper and the History of Its Publication and Reception: A Critical Edition and Documentary Casebook.* Comp. and Ed. Julie Bates Dock. University Park, PA: The Pennsylvania State University Press, 1998. 29–42.

Graff, Gerald. *Beyond the Culture Wars: How Teaching the Conflicts Can Revitalize American Education.* New York: Norton, 1992.

Hedges, Elaine. Afterword. *The Yellow Wallpaper.* New York: The Feminist Press at the City University of New York, 1973. 37–63.

McCormick, Kathleen, Gary Waller, and Linda Flower. *Reading Texts: Reading, Responding, Writing.* Lexington, MA: D.C. Heath & Co., 1987.

Penguin Putnam Inc. American Literature Anthologies for Courses 2000. New York: Penguin Putnam Academic Marketing Department, 2000.

Poe, Edgar Allan. "The Fall of the House of Usher." *Edgar Allan Poe: Selected Prose, Poetry, and Eureka.* Ed. W. H. Auden. New York: Holt, Rinehart and Winston, Inc., 1950.

Steinam, Gloria. "Ruth's Song (Because She Could Not Sing It)." *Outrageous Acts and Everyday Rebellions.* (1983) Rpt. in David Bartholomae and Anthony Petrosky, Eds., *Ways of Reading*, 3rd Edition. Boston: Bedford Books, 1993. 504–22.

Walker, I. M. "The 'Legitimate' Sources of Terror in 'The Fall of the House of Usher.'" (1966) Rpt. in William L. Howarth, Ed., *Twentieth Century Interpretations of Poe's Tales.* Englewood Cliffs, NJ: Prentice-Hall, 1971.

Marjean D. Purinton

READING MARITAL RELATIONSHIPS

The Wallpaper in A Room of One's Own

Introduction: Pedagogical Context for Reading the Wallpaper

In a junior/senior-level course entitled "Women Writers," I teach Charlotte Perkins Gilman's story "The Yellow Wall-paper" (1892). The course emanates from the English Department, but it is cross-listed in our Women's Studies Program, and it usually attracts students, male and female, with cross-disciplinary backgrounds. I fashion this course around the rubric "Relations and Relationships," and we read "The Yellow Wall-paper" during a unit that explores the connections between early twentieth-century efforts at female emancipation and marital relationships. Our exploration considers the ways in which women reading and writing, even women reading about women writing, offer liberating strategies for women entrapped by marriage and heterosexual relationships.

In addition to fostering critical reading skills, analytical writing experiences, and responsible substantive discussion, my objective for this course is to help students discover the conditions under which women wrote at the beginning of the twentieth century and the issues that inform our own "feminist" readings of their works. We reconstruct some of the "oppressions" that characterized women's roles in marriage, family, and society, such as enfranchisement, work outside and inside the home, medical care, marital rape and spousal abuse, contraceptives, child care, child custody, financial independence (credit, loans, property ownership), legal rights (service on juries, power of attorney, power of signature), education, and marital status (single, widowed, divorced, same-sex relationships, sexual desire). Students contribute what they know from other courses and experience, and we make a list of these "oppressions." We also make a list of actual women who were instrumental in improving the conditions of women at the beginning of the twentieth century (e.g., Susan B. Anthony, Sarah Winnemucca, Marie Curie, Anne Sullivan, Dorothea Dix, Harriet Tubman, Ida Tarbell). It is my hope that students will come to appreciate how risky it was for women to discuss these issues openly in their writing and that students will learn to read the subtexts of women's writings so that they can become aware of the ways in which women's writings were at once personal and political.

During this unit, along with "The Yellow Wall-paper," we also read Virginia Woolf's lectures *A Room of One's Own* (1929) and her novel *Mrs. Dalloway* (1925), as well as Susan Glaspell's play *Trifles* (1916) and Lillian Hellman's drama *The Children's Hour* (1934). Situated within the context of these works, then, we discuss what "The Yellow Wall-paper" contributes to women's struggles with marital containment and speculate about what it would mean for women at the turn of the twentieth century to pursue their own desires (Clarissa Dalloway, Karen Wright, Martha Dobie, Gilman's narrator) or their own writing careers (Judith Shakespeare, Virginia Woolf, Gilman's narrator, Charlotte Perkins Gilman) or their own "justice" for abuse (Minnie Wright, Mrs. Hale, Mrs. Peters, Gilman's narrator). Rather than read these works as separate and discrete, I integrate them so that one reading informs the reading of another work. Reading the "wallpaper" in Gilman's story functions as a trope for reading actual and fictional women's lives and for assessing critiques of marital and "compulsory" heterosexual relationships figured by structural and spatial metaphoric relations.[1]

While these are specific texts I have used in this course, it is possible to use Gilman's "Wall-paper" as a trope for reading other texts of this period. The integration of reading texts in the context of actual social and familial issues is a strategy that helps students reach understandings that are not necessarily textually specific. The ideas and activities I share here are easily adaptable to other texts in collaboration with Gilman's "Wall-paper."

Marital issues and abuses exposed in Gilman's story and life are played out but not necessarily resolved in these early twentieth-century writings by women. We therefore brainstorm about how we might read the writing on the wallpaper in the context of the general oppressions that women experienced socially and sexually at the turn of the twentieth century despite political efforts for female equality. At the historical moment when the "Wall-paper" was being written (by both Gilman and her narrator), women were increasingly socially assertive and less passively domesticated as they questioned and defied heterosexist structures that sought to keep them in check. The narrator of "The Yellow Wall-paper" shows us how to read the wallpaper as a text challenging "normative" values and behaviors assigned or reassigned to gender in the context of the period's social and sexual anarchy, a time identified by Clarissa Dalloway as "this late age of the world's experience [which] had bred in them all, all men and women, a well of tears" (13).[2]

Our brainstorming generally results in students identifying the public and private spaces represented by the physical locations of characters and events in the story as well as mental manifestations reflected in the narrative. They point to the layered narration of Gilman's story with its enveloping, rather than linear, structure that circles much like the wallpaper and whose "women" are fuzzy and vague. They see the strategy of peeling off layers of characterization and plot as represented by the peeling patches of the wallpaper. They notice the indeterminate meaning of Gilman's text paralleling the indecipherability of the wallpaper. Gilman's story and the wallpaper invite readers to make meaning, to interact with the story they tell. Much like the relationship between Gilman's narrator and the woman in the wallpaper, readers form a relationship with the text. Both story and wallpaper may not be totally reliable, and students are reminded that they are the products of limited perspectives and from specific times and places. These reading strategies are what we bring to the reading of other texts about relationships.

Our pedagogical context also embraces feminist theoretical perspectives that show us how to read the narrator reading the wallpaper as an act of resistance and transformation.[3] Sometimes students are hesitant to travel into the cognitive and affective territory of readings that expose the fictive nature of social structures they hold to be "true" or "normal," structures from which they uncritically derive selfhood and meaning. They often admonish the abuse dramatized in the Wrights' marriage of *Trifles*, but they are less enthusiastic about examining the heterosexist critiques raised by Clarissa Dalloway's marriage in Woolf's novel or Karen Wright's engagement in *The Children's Hour*. It is important to remind students that we can intellectually explore various theoretical approaches that yield readings and issues that are personally disturbing or uncomfortable without appropriating those positions as a part of our value systems.

Women's writing and feminist perspectives, I point out, enable us to entertain diverse opinions that may test our thinking and compel us to modify our values, or, conversely, may reinforce and strengthen our ways of being. I encourage students to be open-minded, respectful of diverse opinions in their readings and our discussions. Our classroom is a safe space for testing new ideas, a "room of our own" for radical readings. Reading the wallpaper and these texts expose for them the heteropatriarchal ideology ubiquitously operative at the beginning of the twentieth century, an ideology we have inherited as the dominant social structure defining femininity and masculinity. When students can apply tools of feminist analysis, they are then in a better place to suspend their own culturally conditioned beliefs and enter the "what if" mental realm. After all, Woolf reminds us in *A Room of One's Own* that "anything can happen when womanhood has ceased to be a protected occupation" (41).[4]

Pedagogical Approaches and Activities for Reading the Wallpaper

Spatial Relations and Marital Relationships

Marital relationships are figured by spatial dimensions that define and confine women in the writings from this unit. In *A Room of One's Own*, Woolf writes that "a woman must have money and a room of her own if she is to write fiction" (4). The narrator of "The Yellow Wall-paper" has a room of her own but not the financial independence Woolf specifies. Nor is her room a place where she is encouraged to think, to create, to write. The nursery with its "repellent, almost revolting [. . .] smouldering unclean yellow" (31) wallpaper is a space of containment, a place the narrator's husband has recommended to her for a "rest cure," for reconditioning her incipient "feminist" inclinations so that she is returned to her "proper" place in a "compulsory" heterosexual relationship.[5] The narrator's comments about her thinking/writing process hint at ways that her behaviors in the marriage subtly challenge her roles as wife and mother. She questions her will to write and says: "And I know John would think it absurd. But I *must* say what I feel and think in some way—it is such a relief!" (35). The narrator here implies that in her relationship she is not allowed to say what she thinks or feels or that what she thinks and feels is not valued. Is the narrator's relationship with Dr. John more abusive than John Wright's treatment of Minnie, isolated in a "farmhouse kitchen of her own" in Glaspell's play?

Gilman's narrator and Minnie Foster-Wright are divorced from a female community, isolated from women and their connected culture. Their lonesome and insulated spaces are physical and mental prisons, walls upon which they write about their oppression and abuse. Mrs. Hale of *Trifles* reminds her friend and us of how difficult it is to maintain solidarity across differences and distances: "I know how things can be—for women. I tell you, it's queer, Mrs. Peters. We live close together and we live far apart. We all go through the same things—it's all just a different kind of the same thing" (45). We are invited by these women writers to read their "wallpapers," what Gilman's narrator calls her "imaginative power and habit of story-making" (32), alternative texts requiring feminist lenses in order to uncover their painful indictments of the heterosexual relationships that rob them of selfhood, fictions containing the truths about women's lived experiences at the beginning of the twentieth century.

What happens in the spatial confinements of Clarissa Dalloway's Westminster flat of Woolf's novel? Clarissa recounts what it means to be a kind of "madwoman" in the attic[6] and suggests that women discard the imprisoning mental structures that delude them into believing their happiness is derived from marriage: "Like a nun withdrawing, or a child exploring a tower, [Clarissa] went upstairs, paused at the window, came to the bathroom. [. . .] There was an emptiness about the heart of life; an attic room. Women must put off their rich apparel" (45). Clarissa identifies her internalized femininity as a costume to be worn, the proper apparel for married woman, as angel of the house. Similarly, the actual setting of Hellman's drama spatially represents isolated and limited female thinking as femininity-in-training. The Wright-Dobie School for Girls is "a converted farm-house eighteen miles from the town of Lancet" (1.23), geographically distanced from the public sphere. Gilman's narrator, we recall, is taken to an attic room in a "haunted house" (29) "three miles from the village" (30). The women in these writings dramatically convert, although not necessarily successfully or happily, spaces of heteropatriarchal limitations to "rooms of their own," where women might achieve self-actualization, exercise creativity, and live independent of the expectations of heterosexual relationships.

Confined spatially and conceptually by marriage, Clarissa nonetheless endeavors to exercise "that woman's gift, of making a world of her own wherever she happened to be" (114), that is often in a mind of her own and in remembering her "romantic friendship" with Sally Seton. Clarissa reminiscences about love prior to her marriage to Richard Dalloway: "But this question of love (she thought, putting her coat away), this falling in love with women. Take Sally Seton; her relation in the old days with Sally Seton. Had not that, after all, been love?" (48). As Clarissa looks back upon the relationship, she remarks that "the strange thing [. . .] was the purity, the integrity, of her feeling for Sally. It was not like one's feeling for a man. [. . .] It had a quality that could only exist between women" (50). In *The Children's Hour*, Karen Wright and Martha Dobie explore the possibilities for affection outside the limitation of "normative" social patterns. Martha tells Karen: "I've loved you like a friend, the way thousands of women feel about other women" (3.89). Would there be the fictive space, ponders Woolf in *A Room of One's Own*, for a woman, say Mary Carmichael, to write a story in which "Chloe liked Olivia," for "sometimes women do like women"

(86)? We are given some clues about how to read these fictive wallpapers as subversive texts by following the interpretative process of Gilman's narrator who says: "Behind that outside pattern the dim shapes get clearer every day. It is always the same shape, only very numerous. And it is like a woman stooping down and creeping about behind that pattern" (35). She instructs readers to creep around behind the patterns of heteropatriarchal thought and conditioned existence so that women's thinking and pleasures need not be confined by the spatial and cognitive boundaries that seek to contain them.[7]

Two student responses indicate how they applied "reading the wallpaper" strategies suggested by spatial connections to human relations to their own readings. One student writes that both Martha and Karen of Hellman's play "on some levels are unsure of what love really is and what they want out of a relationship and what are appropriate boundaries for their relationship for each other. Once the rumors start, they examine their relationship and its dynamics in a whole new light. Perhaps Karen's marriage could serve as a front or disguise for Karen and Martha's relationship, one marked by mutual sharing and caring." Another student perceptively writes of the importance of women-identified connections and relationships, something the women's spaces facilitate:

> *Mrs. Dalloway* and "The Yellow Wall-paper" depict the need that women have for each other and how their isolation from close relationships with other women has disastrous effects. Clarissa and Sally provide each other with a kind of emotional support, a sense of feeling connected, a unique type of protection that they could not find in their marital relationships. They live life nearly in the same breath, dreaming together and struggling through the challenges that women of this time period faced. The ways in which Clarissa and Sally support each other and encourage each other to be more than society says they can seems to be one of the significant things that the narrator of "The Yellow Wall-paper" lacks. The narrator exposes the many psychological, emotional, and physical constraints of marriage, relational fears and frustrations that John is incapable of understanding. Instead of listening to her, John controls her mind and thoughts, constantly changing her words and feelings to suit his interpretations. His response only deepens her feelings of isolation and loneliness. At the beginning of the story, the narrator describes herself and her husband as "mere ordinary people," a significant statement because it reveals that the dynamics of this marriage could and can be found in many marital relationships in which women are deprived of the emotional support and comforting friendship of other women.

Students made connections between the confinement of actual women to the home, to childbearing, to *restricted* domestic space as something these fictional women were resisting by redefining female spaces and relationships.

Furthermore, they discovered, as did the fictitious characters, that women were beginning to seek a kind of female solidarity over common issues and concerns. A student observed: "Both Johns—of Gilman's story and Glaspell's play—were abusive to wives unconnected to female relationships, isolated from meaningful female contact."

Reading the Pathology of Marriage

The narrator's reading of the wallpaper and our reading of the narrator's reading of the wallpaper reveal fascinating aspects about early twentieth-century culture's reading of woman as the site of psychological disorder and medicine's accompanying notions about the pathology of marriage. While women of the period were inculcated to accept marriage as their *natural* destiny, these writings suggest that patriarchal marriage can be unhealthy, even dangerous, for women. Gilman's narrator is told by her husband-physician that she suffers from a "temporary nervous depression—a slight hysterical tendency" (29), a "false and foolish fancy" (36), a temperament dangerous and fascinating, a condition that makes her unreasonably angry, sensitive, unable to maintain "proper self-control" (30).[8] Her interest in writing links her to a "madness" attributed to women writers of the sixteenth century more loyal to their art than to marital obligations, as Woolf describes in *A Room of One's Own:* "Any woman born with a great gift [. . .] would certainly have gone crazed, shot herself, or ended her days in some lonely cottage outside the village, half witch, half wizard, feared and mocked at. For it needs little skill in psychology to be sure that a highly gifted girl [. . .] must have lost her health and sanity to a certainty" (51). Lucrezia Smith of *Mrs. Dalloway* endures a "madness" inflicted by her marriage to a man suffering from post-war trauma. Septimus Smith has never been his former self since his return from World War I. He hears voices. Septimus says that "people were talking behind the bedroom walls" (99–100) despite Dr. Holmes's diagnosis that there was nothing wrong with him. In marrying Septimus, Lucrezia had given up her home, her friends, her life, but now she had taken off her wedding ring, "the rope was cut" (101), and she was free. We learn from Gilman's narrator that she, too, claims to have a rope secreted in her nursery prison: "I've got a rope up here that even Jennie did not find" (41).

The rope is a recurring image in a number women's writings at the turn of the century—another way of suggesting how their lives were tied to those of men, how their very lives were being strangled out of them, how, in many instances, suicide or homicide seemed to be the only responses to their miseries. Of course, the marriage knot (rope) figures literally as well as figuratively in *Trifles*. Mrs. Wright is driven to madness by the pathology of her marriage, her relationship to an abusive, "hard man" (42), who denied her children, a pet canary, and female companionship. Marriage had changed Minnie from a "sweet and pretty" (43) girl, "kind of timid" (43) to a woman capable of "killing a man while he slept, slipping a rope around his neck that choked the life out of him" (44). The impending marriage of Karen Wright to Dr. Joseph Cardin in Hellman's play, and children's rumors that Karen and Martha Dobie "love" each other impel Martha to confess her love and her guilt about her love to Karen: "I do love you. I resented your marriage; maybe because I wanted you, maybe because I wanted you all along; maybe I couldn't call it by a name; maybe it's been there ever since I first knew you—I never loved a man—I never knew why before" (3.89–90). Feeling "all dirty" (3.90), emotionally unstable, morally responsible for ruining everyone's lives, Martha shoots herself, a surgical suicide in response to cultural limitations on love and relationships. "Wall-paper's" narrator eschews her marital duty, relieved and content when John has "to stay in town over night" (40) and preferring to sleep during the day to avoid lying with John or wishing that her husband "would take another room" (40).[9] Like Minnie Wright, perhaps, the narrator is "a little afraid of John" who "seems very queer sometimes" (37).[10] The "right" marital relationship for these women reduces "femaleness" to a weak, dependent condition, susceptible to hysteria, madness, and evil if not "protected" by husbands who confound male privilege with spousal abuse.

My students were particularly fascinated by these conceptual connections, and some of them related the fictitious women's experiences in marriage with those of actual women of the period, such as Gilman, as well as their own. Many students were surprised that marital relations had not necessarily improved for women during the twentieth century. Spousal abuse, marital rape, childcare, and domestic equality were areas of considerable discussion, as the following students' responses demonstrate. They recognized that now, as in the early twentieth century, women were expected to marry and that marriage itself, with its obligatory child-rearing expectations, often confined women to the home, isolated from other women and their own selfhoods. Women now, as then, battle depression, postpartum depression, and menopausal changes that medicine has yet to address successfully. One student writes: "The narrator of 'The Yellow Wall-paper' exposes the limitation of woman by literally suffering a mental breakdown as a result of her role. A married woman was basically a child who did not possess the privileges of adult males. Gilman's narrator is not taken seriously. Her complaints are regarded as childhood 'boogeyman' nightmares." A graduate student effectively uses the wallpaper as a pattern that informs her reading and analysis as, in this response, she comes to perceive that marriage for some women is a social illness:

The wallpaper is much like the narrator's life—pointless patterns—and she comes to recognize the insanity of patterns John and heteropatriarchal society impose. A pattern that she restructures is the temporal cycle and rhythm associated with conjugal relationships. Femininity is a pattern medicalized as normal sexual behavior for women in the wallpaper, but the narrator experiences more connection to and attraction for the woman/women in the wallpaper. She comes to realize that marriage is not a condition but a position, and she can no longer be contained because she had discovered that her "illness" is actually engendered by socially prescribed relationships.

Reading Woman's Language of Her Own

Reading Gilman's narrator's reading of the wallpaper and her efforts at writing about her reading uncover ways in which women oppressed and repressed in pathological heteropatriarchal relationships struggle to communicate.[11] The narrator shares: "I think sometimes that if I were only well enough to write a little it would relieve the press of ideas and rest me" (32), but her husband forbids her to write, and she must surreptitiously compose her "dead paper" (29), that she is compelled to write, despite the obstacles and her own conflicted feelings about writing. The narrator explains her overwhelming need to share her reading of the wallpaper: "I don't know why I should write this. I don't want to. I don't feel able. And I know John would think it absurd. But I *must* say what I feel and think in some way—it is such a relief!" (34–35). Like Gilman's narrator, Minnie Wright of *Trifles* must communicate in a coded language that only women who read carefully can comprehend. While Gilman's narrator reads and writes herself in the patterns of the wallpaper, Mrs. Wright writes her story in her quilting, a pattern which, Mrs. Hale perceptively observes, is irregular: "Here, this is the one she was working on, and look at the sewing! All the rest of it has been so nice and even. And look at this! It's all over the place! Why, it looks as if she didn't know what she was about!" (41).

Of course, these "papers" invite us to read the female-coded language expressing marital abuse, calling for a social justice denied them by a heteropatriarchal system that silences them. Karen Wright of Hellman's play identifies language's inability to express their incomprehensible situation publicly in the courtroom. She exclaims to her fiancé, Joseph: "And every word will have a new meaning. You think we'll be able to run away from that? Woman, child, love, lawyer—no words that we can use in safety any more. *(Laughs bitterly)* Sick, high-tragic people. That's what we'll be" (3.84). Joseph cannot understand the passionate speech Karen evokes for what appears to him to be a rational explanation. Glaspell's Mr. Hale and Mr. Peters, representatives of law, are similarly unable to read the "trivial" clues of women-centered speech. Like Minnie Wright of *Trifles*, Karen Wright of *The Children's Hour* recognizes the need to tell her story in a language not phallocentric, one that women might share for its expression of injustices they experience in entrapping, marital relationships at the beginning of the twentieth century.

Woolf hopes in *A Room of One's Own* that "in the course of time the mind will be free to write what it likes" (67). The female characters in these texts know that the "course of time" has not yet arrived, and so they "wrote as women write, not as men write" (78), cryptic, concealed, illegible, unrepresentable as they themselves feel in their marital relationships. Clarissa Dalloway finds herself entrapped in the language of her husband: "With a mind of her own, she must always be quoting Richard—as if one couldn't know to a tittle what Richard thought" (116). In contrast, her conversations with Sally are not mimicry: "They sat hour after hour, talking in her bedroom at the top of the house, talking about life, how they were to reform the world. They mean to find a society to abolish private property," and "they spoke of marriage always as a catastrophe" (48, 50). For Gilman's narrator, the woman in the wallpaper could stand in as her "Sally," a female friend with whom she can talk unreservedly and originally about socio-sexual matters in her room "at the top of the house" (30) if the narrator could only free her from the wallpaper. In Woolf's novel, Millicent Burton's devotion to social causes likewise compels her to speak out in the press: "She had to write" (165), but, like married Clarissa, she appropriates the phallocentric language of the public sphere in order to express herself: "After a morning's battle beginning, tearing up, beginning again, she used to feel the futility of her own womanhood as she felt it on no other occasions, and would turn gratefully to the thought of Hugh Whitbread who possessed—no one could doubt it—the art of writing letters to the *Times*" (165).

Woolf's truth-revealing fiction is ironically expressed in Clarissa and Millicent's reluctance to write in a "language of their own." As married women at the beginning of the twentieth century, they become one with their husbands, adopting their names, relying on their language, accepting their own non-being. Woolf's ironic use of language is just as subversive as Minnie Wright's writing in her quilt or as Gilman's narrator's writing on the wall, a resignation that the narrator identifies and simultaneously challenges: "But nobody could climb through that pattern—it strangles so" (Gilman 39). The woman in the wallpaper, Gilman's narrator, and Minnie Wright are being choked, suffocated by "patterns" of marital relationships and phallocentric language. Once women have "broken the sequence—the expected order" (*A Room of One's Own*, 95), as Woolf speculates, writing and reading with "a language of their own," then relational and gender transformations may be possible, as Gilman's narrator exclaims, a female emancipation from patterns in which "you can't put me back!" (42).[12]

Students readily understood the necessity for women writers to develop their own codes and subtexts of communication. One student was especially interested in reading women's silences: "Minnie Wright reminds me of the wife in 'The Yellow Wall-paper' trapped in a 'no-win' situation over the edge by seemingly 'trivial' problems. Both characters escape into their own silences. I can easily imagine women, even today, who cannot breathe because of their overpowering or ignoring mates." Students also connected the imagery of the women's writings with the political activities in which actual women sought equality. Relying on the "rope" image, another student wrote:

> The woman's fascination with the pattern in the wallpaper is symbolic of her own efforts to make sense of her selfhood. In the pattern, she sees an entrapped woman who is trying to escape her prison. The narrator feels more control of this situation because she can pull most of the wallpaper down by herself. She also feels as if she can help free the woman in the pattern. This idea represents the narrator's formation of alternative paths to escape from the control of her husband and patriarchy. She connects with the trapped woman; however, total freedom from the ideals of patriarchy is impossible for Gilman's narrator. Her quest to remove the paper becomes a parallel to the quest of early women's movements. The women had a significant influence in many women's circles and spaces, but the larger society was unconquerable. Faced with defeat, the narrator considers suicide. She has a rope for the woman in the pattern, and she thinks that jumping out the window "would be an admirable exercise."

These student responses reveal how their readings of the subtext, their discoveries of the writings about writings and readings, their identifications of woman-coded language with the wallpaper as a reading trope, increase their sensitivity to the ways in which women writers express cognitive and affective discourse. Their analytical reading skills improved, but they also became excited about discovering in the reading of "The Yellow Wall-paper" ways to read other texts by women. Much to their delight, they often discovered that some texts that seemed too difficult (e.g., novels by Virginia Woolf) or that they just could not find relevant to their lives (e.g., Lillian Hellman's play) were, in fact, much more interesting now that they had some new reading strategies.

Student Activities

Discussion/Writing Questions

Sometimes in a class discussion or in small breakout groups, I pose the following questions to generate informal responses and to stimulate brainstorming for formal essays:

- Describe the spatial, psychological, and marital parallels written on the wallpaper of Gilman's story. How do their "meanings" inform our readings of other women's writings in which we discover spatial, psychological, and marital correspondences?
- Use Chapter Six of *A Room of One's Own* as a framework for reading "The Yellow Wall-paper." How does Woolf's discussion of the difficulties and challenges of the woman writer inform our understanding of Gilman's narrator's need to engage in work that is meaningful to her (writing)? How is "a room of her own" (not) a source of liberation for the narrator? What makes her room "different" from that described by Woolf? What happens to women writers (Woolf, Gilman, the narrator of "The Yellow Wall-paper," Lucrezia Smith) who are married? How do heterosexual relationships inform the writing that these women share? In what ways does their writing direct our readings of their marital relationships?
- In reading the wallpaper of Gilman's story, we see prevailing nineteenth-century notions about the pathology of marriage, including the medicalization of "woman" and "femininity" as a psychological condition. How does the narrator's reading of the woman/pattern in the wallpaper and her own "sickness" contrast with that of the authorized medical profession represented in her husband and brother? How do the narrator's readings and responses inform our readings of the women under medical care in *Mrs. Dalloway* and *The Children's Hour*? What happens to women who do not conform to heterosexual standards of desire and behavior? What happens to their marriages? Who defines social and sexual "illnesses"?
- Consider the episodes in Woolf's novel, Glaspell's play, and Hellman's drama when female characters, like the narrator of "The Yellow Wall-paper," retreat to "a room of their own." Does "a room of their own" give them space to strip to a core self not dressed in socially acceptable costumes? Are their writings alternatives to socially scripted narratives of womanhood? How do these private moments expose the performative nature of gender and the fiction of compulsory heterosexual relationships?
- Does the wallpaper of Gilman's story suggest the possibility of female relationships, even forbidden desires, that are played out more explicitly in the other works? Are women who do not comply with societal expectations seen as "sick"? In what ways do these writings release the woman trapped behind the pattern of the yellow wallpaper, the story's narrator trapped in the pattern of heteropatriarchal marriage and/or phallocentric language?

- Discuss the ways in which Clarissa Dalloway, Karen Wright, Martha Dobie, Minnie Foster-Wright, and Gilman's narrator lose legitimacy and respectability from the circumstances that mark their crises. How are their reputations and senses of self affected by the cultural codes they fail to read and obey?
- Discuss the role of language and silence in "The Yellow Wall-paper," *Mrs. Dalloway*, *Trifles*, and/or *The Children's Hour*. Consider what can and cannot be said by women. Consider the meanings of silence. Consider the ways in which the body has to speak meanings to other women. How do women struggle with self-expression? How does communication affect their marital relationships? How can we read the language that speaks simultaneously within and beyond the boundaries of marriage?
- Clarissa Dalloway and the narrator of "The Yellow Wall-paper" perform identities that are subsumed into those of their husbands. Not willing to accept socially conventional definitions of their sexual selfhood and gendered roles, both women are unhappy in their pathological marriages. What do their struggles, internal and external, reveal about compulsory heterosexist relationships and their effects on women?
- In what ways are we reading something about the lived experiences of Charlotte Perkins Gilman, Virginia Woolf, Susan Glaspell, and Lillian Hellman in reading their works, depictions of fictional women writing and reading? How do the lived experiences of these writers inform our readings of their fictions? In what ways are the lived and fictional experiences useful in our reading of the sociopolitical conditions influencing women at the beginning of the twentieth century? [Note: You will need to do some research for this question—reference biographies, autobiographies, and diaries/journals.][13]

Group Work and Creative Projects

Since I operate with shared leadership and decentralized authority in this course, students perceive our class as an educational "space of their own" in which they participate in their own discovery process. For creative projects, I invite students to do a "readers' theatre" of a segment of a text or, in the case of *Trifles* and *The Children's Hour*, especially, stage a representative scene. In both instances, students need to set up the scene, to point to its importance, to explain how reading the wallpaper of Gilman's story informs the reading they are performing, and then after the "performance," to facilitate a group discussion.

Another project involves students assuming various fictive characters ("Wall-paper's" narrator and Dr. John, Clarissa and Richard Dalloway, Minnie and John Wright, Mrs. and Mr. Hale, Mrs. and Mrs. Peters, Sally Seton, Millicent Burton, Karen Wright, Martha Dobie, and Dr. Joseph Cardin, Chloe and Olivia) and then staging a roundtable discussion of how their relationships have shaped their lives. Students may perform cross-gendered or transvestite roles. Prior to their discussion, students work up a set of questions or issues that they will agree to cover so that they can prepare their "roles." Students also enjoy a project requiring them to adopt the persona of "Wall-paper's" narrator and then write a "review" of one of the other four texts. They are positioned by this exercise to read through the lens of the narrator who is reading the wallpaper, an exercise that demands their analysis of the "Wall-paper" narrator before they can interpret another reading from her perspective.[14]

Because I want students to experience collaborative and cross-disciplinary work, they are required to make one group presentation. In addition to those which I have already shared, students can also organize their presentation around a TV news magazine or talk-show format, teach a class using an interactive format (especially useful for students seeking education certification), hold a debate, create a mock academic conference panel (particularly good for graduate students who might be taking the course), script an interview with fictional characters or actual writers, adopt a text for their own dramatic or cinematic presentation, or create a visual documentary. The students in this course generate the most creative and analytically sophisticated group presentations that I have experienced at the undergraduate level.

Conclusion

My goal is for students to come away from this course reading "differently," and "The Yellow Wall-paper" helps them to achieve new ways of reading and thinking about fiction written by women. They discover the connections between actual women's lives and those of fictional women reflected in the literature. They perceive what benefits they enjoy from the work of their foremothers and what work remains for them and future feminists to accomplish in terms of women's conditions. What they read becomes accessible and relevant. They learn from each other in collaborative activities that they find fun as well as challenging. At the end of the semester, I ask them to reflect upon what important "things" they have learned, what piece of literature was most interesting, most memorable, most useful to them. "The Yellow Wall-paper" is frequently cited precisely because it helped them to read other texts by women. Their close textual readings are enriched by an understanding of the larger social contexts in which women's writing emerges. While we have focused on women's relations and relationships (because these texts were especially useful for that organizing rubric), they can apply these skills and knowledge to other learning experiences. Many of the students who take this course are pursuing teaching certification, and they indicate to me that the approaches we have taken to women's writing will help them in their own teaching of literature.[15]

Notes

1. Students unfamiliar with literary theory will find it helpful to consult Adrienne Rich's seminal 1980 essay "Compulsory Heterosexuality and Lesbian Existence."
2. My critical and pedagogical perspectives are informed by Annette Kolodny's "A Map for Reading: Or, Gender and the Interpretation of Literary Texts"; Judith Fetterley's "Reading About Reading: 'A Jury of her Peers,' 'The Murders in the Rue Morgue,' and 'The Yellow Wallpaper'"; and Mary Jacobus's "An Unnecessary Maze of Sign-Reading."
3. See, for example, Richard Feldstein, "Reader, Text, and Ambiguous Referentiality in 'The Yellow Wall-Paper"; Julian Wolfreys, *The Rhetoric of Affirmative Resistance: Dissonant Identities from Carroll to Derrida;* and Ruth Robbins, "Reading the Writing on the Wall: Charlotte Perkins Gilman's 'The Yellow Wall-paper,'" which adopt a variety of feminist theoretical approaches.
4. For the purpose of this pedagogical essay, all quotations from the primary sources reflect my classroom teaching texts with the exception of the edition of Gilman's "The Yellow Wall-paper."
5. Heather Kirk Thomas's provocative analysis of late-nineteenth-century interior decorations as strategies for displacing women's domestic empowerment offers another way of reading the wallpaper in the context of "feminine spaces" and marital relationships. Anne Heilmann asserts that Gilman visualizes her emerging feminist opposition to the "pointless pattern" of male thought and cultural production; see 175–88.
6. Sandra M. Gilbert and Susan Gubar's seminal study *The Madwoman in the Attic: The Woman Writer and the Nineteenth-Century Literary Imagination* points out the parallel between Gilman's narrator's recourse to her attic room and the imprisonment in the "infected house" of her own maternal body, 88–92.
7. Barbara Johnson offers an alternative reading of the wallpaper as an education in female passivity, a narrative of the narrator's growing complicity in her own destruction and madness, "Is Female to Male as Ground Is to Figure?," 255–68. Catherine J. Golden, on the other hand, reads the theatrical conclusion of Gilman's story as one which dramatically reverses, albeit temporarily, the dynamics of gender in the narrator's choice of literal madness over docility and obedience implicated in John's cure, "Caging the Beast: The Radical Treatment for 'Excessive Maleness' in Gilman's Fiction," 122–34.
8. Numerous studies develop the medical/paternal and psychological/patriarchal analysis implied in this reading, for example, Berman, Treichler, and Masse.
9. I am grateful to P. J. Mann, a graduate student in our interdisciplinary Masters program, whose conversational observations about the conjugal pattern depicted in "The Yellow Wall-Paper" reified my own sense that the narrator increasingly avoids sexual contact with her husband. It is also interesting that the narrator adds to her aversion of her husband's sleeping with her a rejection of female bed-sharing: "Jennie wanted to sleep with me—the sly thing!—but I told her I should undoubtedly rest better for a night all alone" (40). For a queer consideration of this line, see Crewe in this volume.

10. Jonathan Crewe develops the repressed same-sex desire expressed perversely, symptomatically, self-destructively, in the story's pathologization of women's minds and bodies by conjugal-medical authority in his "Queering 'The Yellow Wallpaper'? Charlotte Perkins Gilman and the Politics of Form."
11. See Carol Thomas Neely, "Alternative Women's Discourse," 315–22; Karen Ford, "'The Yellow Wallpaper' and Women's Discourse," 309–14; Paula A. Treichler, "The Wall Behind the Yellow Wallpaper: Response on Carol Neely and Karen Ford," 323–30; Jean E. Kennard, "Convention Coverage or How to Read Your Own Life," 69–88; Ann J. Lane, "What My Therapist, My Daughter, and Charlotte Taught Me While I Was Writing the Biography of Charlotte Perkins Gilman," 27–34 for variations on this reading of the wallpaper.
12. It is important to note Susan Lanser's perceptive observation that the immensely complicated text of Gilman's story and its wallpaper remain incompletely read, and she cautions us against reading both as universalized, essentialized women's texts that can be deciphered.
13. For Gilman, in particular, I direct students to *The Living of Charlotte Perkins Gilman: An Autobiography; The Diaries of Charlotte Perkins Gilman;* Mary A. Hill, *Charlotte Perkins Gilman: The Making of a Radical Feminist 1860–1896;* Gary Scharnhorst, *Charlotte Perkins Gilman;* Ann J. Lane, *To "Herland" and Beyond: The Life and Work of Charlotte Perkins Gilman*. Also useful, Charlotte Perkins Gilman, *Herland*, which students probably read in the Introduction to Women's Studies course, and *Women and Economics: A Study of the Economic Relation Between Men and Women as a Factor in Social Evolution*, especially for graduate students as well as the background documents and criticisms available in *The Captive Imagination: A Casebook on* The Yellow Wall-Paper and the manuscript information in Julie Bates Dock's edition of "The Yellow Wall-paper."
14. It might be helpful for graduate students or interested advanced students to look at feminist readings of "The Yellow Wall-paper" including, Denise D. Knight, *Charlotte Perkins Gilman: A Study of the Short Fiction;* Elaine B. Hedges, "'Out at Last'? 'The Yellow Wallpaper' after Two Decades of Feminist Criticism," and "Afterword" to "The Yellow Wall-Paper" by Charlotte Perkins Gilman.
15. I wish to thank Jeffrey Weinstock for his helpful comments on versions of this essay.

Works Cited

Berman, Jeffrey. "The Unrestful Cure: Charlotte Perkins Gilman and 'The Yellow Wallpaper.'" *The Captive Imagination: A Casebook on* The Yellow Wallpaper. Ed. Catherine Golden. New York: The Feminist Press, 1992. 211–41.

Crewe, Jonathan. "Queering 'The Yellow Wallpaper'? Charlotte Perkins Gilman and the Politics of Form." *Tulsa Studies in Women's Literature* 14.2 (Fall 1995): 273–93.

Dock, Julie Bates, Comp. and Ed. *Charlotte Perkins Gilman's "The Yellow Wall-paper" and the History of Its Publication and Reception: A Critical Edition and Documentary Casebook.* University Park, PA: The Pennsylvania State University Press, 1998.

Feldstein, Richard. "Reader, Text, and Ambiguous Referentiality in 'The Yellow Wallpaper.'" *Feminism and Psychoanalysis.* Eds. Richard Feldstein and Judith Roof. Ithaca: Cornell University Press, 1989. 269–79.

Ford, Karen. "'The Yellow Wallpaper' and Women's Discourse." *Tulsa Studies in Women's Literature* 4.2 (1985): 309–14.

Gilbert, Sandra M., and Susan Gubar. *The Madwoman in the Attic: The Woman Writer and the Nineteenth-Century Literary Imagination*. New Haven: Yale University Press,1979.

Gilman, Charlotte Perkins. *The Diaries of Charlotte Perkins Gilman*. Ed. Denise D. Knight. Charlottesville: University Press of Virginia, 1994. 2 vols.

——. *Herland*. 1915. New York: Pantheon, 1979.

——. *The Living of Charlotte Perkins Gilman: An Autobiography*. New York: C. Appleton-Century, 1935 Madison: University of Wisconsin Press, 1990.

——. *Women and Economics: A Study of the Economic Relation Between Men and Women as a Factor in Social Evolution*. 1898. Berkeley: University of California Press, 1998.

——. Gilman, Charlotte Perkins. "The Yellow Wallpaper." 1892. *Charlotte Perkins Gilman's "The Yellow Wall-paper" and the History of Its Publication and Reception: A Critical Edition and Documentary Casebook*. Comp. and Ed. Julie Bates Dock. University Park, PA: The Pennsylvania State University Press, 1998. 29–42.

Glaspell, Susan. *Trifles*. 1916. *Plays by Susan Glaspell*. Ed. C. W. E. Bigsby. Cambridge: Cambridge University Press, 1991. 35–45.

Golden, Catherine, Ed. *The Captive Imagination: A Casebook on* The Yellow Wallpaper. New York: The Feminist Press, 1992.

Golden, Catherine J. "Caging the Beast: The Radical Treatment for 'Excessive Maleness' in Gilman's Fiction." *The Mixed Legacy of Charlotte Perkins Gilman*. Ed. Catherine J. Golden and Joanna Schneider Zangrando. Newark: University of Delaware Press, 2000. 122–34.

Hedges, Elaine B. "'Out at Last?' 'The Yellow Wallpaper' after Two Decades of Feminist Criticism." *The Captive Imagination: A Casebook on* The Yellow Wallpaper. Ed. Catherine Golden. New York: The Feminist Press, 1992. 313–33.

——. "Afterword." *"The Yellow Wallpaper" by Charlotte Perkins Gilman*. Rev. ed. New York: The Feminist Press, 1996. 37–62.

Heilmann, Anne. "Overwriting Decadence: Charlotte Perkins Gilman, Oscar Wilde, and the Feminization of Art in 'The Yellow Wall-paper'." *The Mixed Legacy of Charlotte Perkins Gilman*. Ed. Catherine J. Golden and Joanna Schneider Zangrando. Newark: University of Delaware Press, 2000. 175–88.

Hellman, Lillian. *The Children's Hour*. 1934. *Plays by and About Women*. Eds. Victoria Sullivan and James Hatch. New York: Random House, 1974. 19–96.

Hill, Mary A. *Charlotte Perkins Gilman: The Making of a Radical Feminist, 1860–1896*. Philadelphia: Temple University Press, 1980.

Jacobus, Mary. "An Unnecessary Maze of Sign-Reading." *Reading Woman: Essays in Feminist Criticism*. New York: Columbia University Press, 1986. 229–48.

Johnson, Barbara. "Is Female to Male as Ground Is to Figure?" *Feminism and Psychoanalysis*. Eds. Richard Feldstein and Judith Roof. Ithaca: Cornell University Press, 1989. 255–68.

Kennard, Jean E. "Convention Coverage or How to Read Your Own Life." *New Literary History* 13.1 (1989): 69–88.

Kolodny, Annette. "A Map for Reading: Or, Gender and the Interpretation of Literary Texts." *New Literary History* 11.3 (Spring 1980): 451–67.

Knight, Denise D. *Charlotte Perkins Gilman: A Study of the Short Fiction*. New York: Twayne, 1997.

Lane, Ann J. "What My Therapist, My Daughter, and Charlotte Taught Me While I Was Writing the Biography of Charlotte Perkins Gilman." *The Mixed Legacy of Charlotte Perkins Gilman*. Eds. Catherine J. Golden and Joanna Schneider Zangrando. Newark: University of Delaware Press, 2000. 27–34.

——. *To "Herland" and Beyond: The Life and Work of Charlotte Perkins Gilman*. New York: Pantheon, 1990.

Lanser, Susan. "Feminist Criticism, 'The Yellow Wallpaper,' and the Politics of Color in America." *Feminist Studies* 15.3 (1989): 415–41.

Masse, Michelle A. *In the Name of Love: Women, Masochism, and the Gothic*. Ithaca: Cornell University Press, 1992.

Neely, Carol Thomas. "Alternative Women's Discourse." *Tulsa Studies in Women's Literature* 4.2 (1985): 315–22.

Rich, Adrienne. "Compulsory Heterosexuality and Lesbian Existence." *Blood, Bread, and Poetry: Selected Prose 1979–1985*. New York: Norton, 1986. 23–75.

Robbins, Ruth. "Reading the Writing on the Wall: Charlotte Perkins Gilman's 'The Yellow Wallpaper.'" *Literary Feminisms*. New York: St. Martin's, 2000. 242–58.

Scharnhorst, Gary. *Charlotte Perkins Gilman*. Boston: Twayne, 1985.

Thomas, Heather Kirk. "[A] Kind of 'debased Romanesque' with *delirium tremens:* Late-Victorian Wall Coverings and Charlotte Perkins Gilman's 'The Yellow Wallpaper'." *The Mixed Legacy of Charlotte Perkins Gilman*. Eds. Catherine J. Golden and Joanna Schneider Zangrando. Newark: University of Delaware Press, 2000. 189–206.

Treichler, Paula A. "Escaping the Sentence: Diagnosis and Discourse in 'The Yellow Wallpaper.'" *Tulsa Studies in Women's Literature* 3.1–2 (1984): 61–77.

——. "The Wall Behind the Yellow Wallpaper: Response on Carol Neely and Karen Ford." *Tulsa Studies in Women's Literature* 4.2 (1985): 323–30.

Wolfreys, Julian. *The Rhetoric of Resistance: Dissonant Identities from Carroll to Derrida*. London: Macmillan, 1997.

Woolf, Virginia. *Mrs. Dalloway*. 1925. San Diego: Harcourt Brace, 1975.

——. *A Room of One's Own*. 1929. San Diego: Harcourt Brace, 1973.

Paul Reifenheiser

INTERPRETIVE BONDAGE

Reader Response, Authorial Intention, and Gilman's "The Yellow Wall-paper"

Students in introductory college literature courses often feel as trapped as the narrator of Charlotte Perkins Gilman's "The Yellow Wall-paper." Some undergraduates have internalized the idea that a text has "one" meaning and that determining authorial intention provides the best method for its discovery. Others realize the problems with authorial intention but leave the "correct" interpretations to critics, scholars, and their teachers. Either way, numerous students find themselves surrounded by the ideas of others and forget to look within themselves and the classroom community for possible interpretations. These issues can become magnified when teaching mandatory introductory literature courses to predominantly non-English majors. Non-English majors often have less exposure to literary theory; they may be more willing to accept a classroom environment that imposes meaning rather than one that invites individualized responses to literature. Thus, introductory courses, filled mostly with non-English majors, sometimes require more discussion of the dangers of interpretive bondage than upper-level courses. To free students from this interpretive prison, a teacher must disabuse them of the fallacious notion that stories have only one meaning, that their own interpretations are not valid, and that their role in the class is to listen to a teacher lecture about possible correct meanings in fiction. In order to thwart students from seeking all their answers from the pedagogue, teachers must diffuse authority throughout the classroom. The texts we choose facilitate this process, especially complex works that invite numerous approaches and reach students on multiple levels. Gilman's "The Yellow Wall-paper" offers an excellent resource for this reader-response approach to teaching because it invites students, teachers, and critics to interpret it on individual levels. However, its difficulty disallows its readers from indulging in hubris stemming from the belief that they control all its meanings. This pedagogical style can be daunting for those in a very common classroom situation: non-Gilman scholars teaching the often-anthologized story to students who are not English majors. Teachers in this situation must hurdle the following two obstacles: first, they must overcome firmly entrenched beliefs that the interpretation of literature is best left to the experts and not students; second, non-Gilman scholars must develop a firm understanding of the interpretative history of the story.

Not only can a student easily apply a reader-response approach to "The Yellow Wall-paper," but a pedagogue also may use the text as an excellent device to introduce students to the validity of this interpretive methodology. A careful analysis of the story and its history reveals the problems with Gilman's own recorded intention for the story (rebuking authorial intention) and the fractured evolution of interpretations by critics, especially feminist critics, since the story's reprinting in 1973 (removing the idea that critics agree on singular meanings). Although commonplace within the academic community, these ideas may surprise and startle students new to literature and literary criticism. Pedagogues cannot simply tell their students about these issues; they must show the value of reader-response as well as the problems with critical authority and authorial intention. A teacher who dictates meanings to students through static lectures and asks them only to memorize and reproduce them for tests and papers can create a stifling atmosphere. In this environment students fail to use critical thinking skills, jettison original interpretations based out of their own experiences, and do not teach the professor and each other through their own readings. Unfortunately, some students often crave this setting because memorizing meanings can be easier than developing original thoughts. Thus, students hold varying attitudes towards learning: some crave conformity and stability, while others wish to challenge traditional styles through creative modes. Effective teachers encourage that creative freedom, while oppressive teachers seek to squelch original expression and facilitate student conformity.

In my introductory short story class, I teach "The Yellow Wall-paper" as one of the first stories because it helps to create an atmosphere in which students develop original interpretations and help teach each other, including myself, throughout the semester. In my course, I open with a brief discussion of pedagogical objectives, including issues concerning authorial intention, reader response in the classroom, student relationships to both authors and published critics, and research paper and journal assignments that ask them to become their own critics. I follow this introduction by applying these basic principles to Gilman's famous short story. In this essay, I use the same basic format.

Removing students from interpretive bondage takes numerous steps. The notion that an author controls all forms of interpretation through his or her stated intentions represents the first shackle from which students must gain freedom. A common misconception holds that comparing the work to the intent of its author remains the best way to determine the value of a story. When "other" interpretations seem to go "too far," some students make statements like: "I don't think the author meant that when she wrote this" or "Gilman couldn't have possibly meant for this story to be read with homosexual undertones." Within the first week of the semester, we discuss this concept and the value of authorial intention. Wimsatt and Beardsley's landmark essay "The Intentional Fallacy" provides a starting point but has its problems as well. In this essay, these New Critics remove the author from the interpretation process and focus their attention solely on the text. Such a move only switches the keys of the students' interpretive prison from the author to the critic. As E. D. Hirsch states, "If the author had been banished, the critic still remained, and his new, original, urbane, ingenious, or relevant 'reading' carried its own interest" (13). Such a switch still removes students from the field of interpretation, and it makes them what Paulo Freire calls receptacles of knowledge waiting to be filled by the almighty critic and/or professor, who "makes deposits which the students patiently receive, memorize, and repeat" (53). Although Freire discusses the abuse of power in the educational system of Third World countries, many students find similar circumstances of "banking" in high school or college classes whenever a teacher forces on students the "one" meaning of a text. Some may consider this a minor abuse of power, but it contributes to a systemic limiting of options that continues to plague those oppressed throughout the world. Through an in-class analysis of Freire, I try to question authorial intention, to connect my students and those outside of our classroom, and to establish a link between students and the narrator of "The Yellow Wall-paper."

More sophisticated arguments for critiquing intention exist, but I find the following three sufficient for introductory literature or short story classes: first, the stated intention often does not exist; second, even if the intention does exist, it may prove false, ambiguous, or changing over time; third, while authors manipulate language to tell stories, they do not own language and cannot control how others will interpret the words they have chosen. Students must understand the difficulty in finding stated intentions, the impossibility of absolutely verifying them, and, even if found and trusted, the problem with privileging them more than other careful readings. I use these three points not to remove the author's intention, if available, but to allow students to realize that it becomes one of many interpretations, including their own. I ask students to seek authors' intentions but not to consider them the only correct or the one true meaning of their stories.

The reduction of the author's power must not simply shift the balance to the critic. Such an endeavor leaves students trapped but by a different master. The keys to interpretive freedom lie in making students see themselves as critics. When students find themselves trapped beneath the authority of the author and that of the critic, freedom comes from collapsing the entire interpretive structure; removing just one part fails to end students' bondage. Reader response allows critics, the author, and undergraduates equal access to a text. Each one becomes another reader or, as I like to put it to my students, they all become critics. Even students who do not consider themselves adept at interpreting texts can take part in the conversation because they can "intertwine their life experiences, the experiences in the text, and the experiencing of the text in order to comprehend the reading and to understand their own lives as well" (Buckler 46). If students must always defer to the author or to a published critic, then they are decidedly out of the conversation. Such a position runs the risk of alienating students and making the readings foreign bodies to which they cannot relate in any capacity. Enforcing specific meanings on them limits the power of the texts we assign.

E. D. Hirsch offers an important counter-argument to this position of indeterminacy by noting that if one interpretation is as valid as another, then the teacher has no "firm ground" on which to claim that his reading is more valid than a pupil's reading. He contends, "this impasse is a principal cause of the loss of bearings sometimes felt though not often confessed by academic critics" (13). Hirsch's argument assumes that a teacher feels the need to be "more valid" than the other members of the classroom community. Allowing students to delve into their own interpretations does not have to threaten the authority of the teacher. Pedagogues can provide readings that they and published critics privilege, while still allowing students the freedom and flexibility to explore their own options. The seeming indeterminacy Hirsch fears becomes an enormous advantage to the teacher of college literature courses who wants to spread authority throughout the class, especially when teaching non-majors who often feel that they lack effective interpretive skills. Possible assignments and interpretations of "The Yellow Wall-paper" (listed later in this essay) offer examples of this advantage.

David Bleich writes, "If we acquire the courage to eschew our patronizing task of 'introducing' students to 'our' style of study, and instead ask all our students, younger or older, to introduce their own ways and thoughts for mutual sharing, we will have begun a productive response to the many voices now seeking to educate for an authentically just society" (21–22). This courage must begin at the start of the semester. An important step lies in not dwelling too long on the specific theoretical relationship between the text and the reader. Steven Mailloux calls for a rhetorical hermeneutics that moves beyond simple questions about whether the text or the reader determines interpretation. Instead rhetorical hermeneutics collapses the distinction because it "claims there is no way of theoretically describing the correct reader-text relation in general" (Mailloux 52). He calls this approach therapeutic because it moves beyond regulating claims. From a teaching perspective, it liberates a professor from probing too deeply into communication theory concerning the text and reader that may be difficult. The focus then turns from how interpretation works to "how interpretive practices function within sociopolitical contexts of persuasion. These contexts involve tropes and arguments within the cultural conversation at specific historical moments" (52–53). All students bring some access to a community and a specific historical moment of their own to the classroom. This individual access to a cultural conversation provides the foundation for their interpretive authority, and reading becomes "a coming together, a convention" (Kennard 86). Since each student offers distinct community experiences, it holds that students may then create a classroom community where students learn from each other, thus further blurring the line between teacher, critic, and student.

Journal assignments, in-class activities, and a research paper assignment all augment this sense of community. Shared journal assignments have students thinking through similar questions and issues prior to class discussion. In-class activities focused through small group discussions give students, especially those nervous about speaking in large groups, the opportunity to both listen and respond to other students within their community. This sense of engagement underpins the entire reader-response approach, and it offers a clear model to follow when researching the texts on which they will write their research paper. Expecting students to create their own critical interpretations throughout the semester yields tremendous fruit when assigning research papers. The process of researching published interpretations of literature and applying creative and interesting perspectives produces excellent papers. By expecting students to create their own ideas and make original connections, students write interesting research papers rather than dull research reports, which are often boring for students to write and for professors to read.

The research paper becomes the culmination of a student's quest to become a critic. I expect them to enter the critical conversation by engaging with other critics, but I want them to strive for their own original space. I invite them to apply their own experiences to the texts and to remember that being original doesn't have to mean creating some "earth-shattering" interpretation of the text. I encourage them to look to their cultural circumstances and texts that surround them and use them as lenses through which to interpret the literary texts we discuss. Thus, everything around them becomes a text open to interpretation and to some form of reader response. This element of intertextuality offers endless options for the paper. With all things open to interpretation and interconnected through the students, the course offers another means to see that enforced limitations (or issues unavailable to interpretation) bear the possibility of oppression both in their classroom and cultural community. The writing of their papers offers students an entrance to the community of critics and provides a release for their own interpretations, and the narrator's journal in "The Yellow Wall-paper" offers a union with a previously forbidden and creative realm. Rather than requiring students to write a tedious assignment, the paper becomes an exercise where students may express themselves freely. Still, some students resist this freedom because it necessitates more responsibility and work than simply doing as they are told. The value of this freedom must find its way into the classroom through the texts we assign, and Gilman's story functions brilliantly on this level.

Gilman's "The Yellow Wall-paper" provides a means to discuss a wide range of theoretical issues, but I use it mostly to discuss reader response because it offers students a tangible example of the problems with using authorial intention as the best means for interpreting a text. Since an enormous amount of work lacks stated authorial intention, most students see that flaw as obvious. However, Gilman's story offers an excellent illustration of a text for which the recorded intention of the author exists but has come under scrutiny. Julie Bates Dock's casebook on "The Yellow Wall-paper" provides an excellent starting point for non-Gilman scholars who are researching the text for their courses. In a 1913 essay in *The Forerunner*, Gilman writes that the story "was not intended to drive people crazy, but to save people from being driven crazy, and it worked" (86). In her 1935 autobiography, Gilman writes "But the real purpose of the story was to reach Dr. S. Weir Mitchell, and convince him of the error of his ways" (88). Numerous problems with these proclaimed intentions exist.

The first and most obvious problem concerns the element of time. The stated intentions follow the story by nearly fifteen and forty years, respectively.

This lapse in time allowed Gilman ample opportunity to alter or dismiss previous beliefs about the story; an analysis of her statements supports the possibility of this hypothesis. In both the essay and her autobiography, Gilman mentions a doctor from Boston who wrote to *The Transcript* protesting her story. She used this letter, one from a doctor in Kansas, and hearsay about S. Weir Mitchell to establish that the male-dominated medical profession had problems with her story. In her autobiography Gilman reproduces the Boston letter, signed "M.D.," for her audience. Julie Bates Dock writes, "With the letter reprinted nicely before us, surely we can trust Gilman's own account. Or can we? A look at the *Transcript* for 8 April 1892 challenges Gilman's cry of male censorship as well as the scholarly depictions that derive from it" (Dock 21). Not relying on Gilman's reproduction of the Boston letter, Dock used the original copy in *The Transcript.* She found spaces in between the letters "M" and "D" where Gilman had placed the two letters together. The space reveals that the letters could represent a person's initials rather than an indication of a medical doctor. Dock notes that critics who have relied on Gilman's own account "have missed the opportunity to consider how Gilman's expectations or motives might have colored her own perception and transmission of the letter" (Dock 21–22). Gilman may have fabricated her intentions in an attempt to discredit the medical profession that she believed, or wanted to believe, attacked her story. However, that attack may not have been as widespread as Gilman wanted or believed.

Concerning "The Yellow Wall-paper," Dale M. Bauer writes, "the story stresses Gilman's primary commitment to social reform and to changing the world in concrete ways rather than to the production of lasting artistic works" (347). This, in part, may explain why Gilman only claimed that the story was an attempt to discredit S. Weir Mitchell. By 1935, S. Weir Mitchell's rest cure had fallen out of fashion, and Gilman could charge that her story represented an important part of the reason for that fall. Her desire for the story to have a concrete effect could have swayed her from admitting that the story was more than an attack on the rest cure. Gilman was an outspoken writer concerning the economic problems of marriage, and "The Yellow Wall-paper" might have constituted too vague an attack on marriage or patriarchy for her to find it useful in that regard. She may have tried to limit its interpretation by advancing a more focused and, from her perspective, a more socially useful reading. A similar desire for a text to have an important effect often influences students' reception of works as well. Sometimes students want the story to work on a specific social level because that holds more value to them than a story that primarily entertains. The introduction of differing views on how the text works creates a foundation for classroom discussion that authorial intention often gainsays. More importantly, students' perceptions of a story often change with time, including between a first and second reading or over the few months that comprise a semester. Such a realization helps students understand that authors do not have immunity from this same action for their own work. Like critics and students assessing a work, the stated intentions of authors may change as their interpretation of their work grows with time. The author and the reader suddenly seem closer than some students realize.

Since its publication, critics have read the story as holding something other than a simple critique of S. Weir Mitchell. It has been read as a gothic story, but, as Dock notes, contemporary reviews also "demonstrate that the story's first readers did recognize its indictments of marriage and of the treatment of women, even if they did not label them with modern terms like 'sexual politics'" (19). Gilman may have masked her original intentions within the rest cure attack for fear that a male-dominated press would not have published or received it well otherwise. This would lend credence to the notion that authors sometimes must hide their true intentions for fear that their work will not find publishers or for fear of retribution. Students sometimes fail to consider that political, cultural, and economic forces often cause authors to alter their specific intentions. Students frequently find themselves in a similar situation when they fear that disagreeing with a teacher will harm their grade or invite scorn from their instructors. I actively encourage my students to disagree respectfully with me and others in the class in order to create an open environment. This potential for disagreement diffuses authority and helps students feel more involved in the course. Early in the semester I inform students that I will challenge their positions to help them think through issues, but I am not in a position to tell students that their interpretations are wrong simply because I disagree with them. This simple message frees students to interact with each other and myself more regularly. Gilman may not have had that same freedom when considering a publisher for her text.

Gilman's desire may have always been to critique Mitchell and nothing more, but the circumstances still provide questions about her stated intentions. Students need to realize that we simply don't know if her stated intentions were truthful or altered since the time of the writing. Gilman's letters and discussions of her story remain as open to interpretation as the story itself. While her stated intentions may offer some insight, they simply cannot work as a vehicle for finding the "one" meaning of the story. Gilman's stated intention also severely limits the text. Her letters show a problem with the rest cure, but she never shows concern for the fact that Mitchell used one version of the cure for men and a more restricted version for women. In merely attacking Mitchell and his rest cure, she never delves into anything directly gender related. Limiting the story to a critique of an antiquated form of therapy makes the text a relic, thus lessening the ability for contemporary readers to make connections. Critical views open the scope of the text and allow the story to transcend barriers of time. "The Yellow Wall-paper" forces students to realize that critics often advance interpretations of stories that offer potentially more fruitful avenues of exploration than stated intentions by an author. Students who find this notion untenable sometimes fail to recognize that language is a social construct; authors have little control over subconscious or possibly unintended usages that may exist in their stories and letters. They cannot control the complexity of the language they employ. Thus readers/critics have the authority to formulate their own interpretations of that language. Gilman's famous story creates an excellent forum for introducing these fundamental lessons about interpreting literature. This approach liberates students and allows them to find individualized interpretations of works written well before their birth. This possibility belies the often-held notion that students can only relate to contemporary texts. Gilman's work remains vibrant to students over a century after its publication because critics revived its place in the canon and because students may continually breath new life into it with each rereading.

Students must realize that critics also have varying ties to cultural and historical communities. Elaine Hedges writes that critical interpretations of "The Yellow Wall-paper" stem from an historical moment when "there was a community of readers sharing the same literary conventions, the same expectations of woman's literature, and, I would add, the same political hopes" (229–230). This critical community of feminist scholars holds important similarities to a classroom of students. Scholars will most likely approach the story with more experience reading and interpreting literature, but that does not guarantee a consensus. Disagreements based on gender, economics, race, and other variables develop in both critical and classroom communities.[1] This allows the teacher to present critical interpretations as important vehicles for discovery but not as the only ones available. Professors may use the fluidity of scholarly investigation to teach specific approaches without stifling students' own creative interpretations. For example, I am weary of opening a discussion by simply asking students what they thought of a text. I prefer a less generalized prompt to start a conversation, but I usually use this broad opening during a class on "The Yellow Wall-paper." Since it is early in the semester and because the text is varied and challenging, I find it valuable to survey the room and students' approaches to the text. I usually keep my commentary to a minimum at this point, take in what the students offer, and recall it later when we focus on more specific parts of the text. This move is both symbolic and substantive because the approach gives students the first chance to discuss the text before I entertain any published critical thought. Later, students can weave their interpretations in with those of the published critics, especially those advanced by feminist scholars.

Despite its early reception and notoriety, the feminist readings of the past 30 years have placed the story permanently in the canon of U.S. literature. Undoubtedly this incredibly influential feminist criticism represents the starting point for an examination of "The Yellow Wall-paper." Critics cite Gilman's desire to confront the rest cure but add, "to read it this way is to efface the story's imaginative power, so that it becomes almost the kind of rational document that the husband himself could commend" (King and Morris 24). This statement opens the door to feminist readings by challenging Gilman's intent as being a product of oppressive patriarchy. I focus on one specific approach to the text, already advanced by critics, as a critical point that allows feminist readings to coexist with other possible interpretations. However, in the classroom, I very clearly emphasize that the reading I use represents one of many plausible interpretations, and I invite them to challenge it at every turn. Throughout discussion I repeat that it offers a foundation for a critical edifice, and I stress that this interpretation—like any other—is something upon which we can build, not a static structure. Through this caveat, I remind students that we will engage other interpretations in our conversations, but we will seek to augment them with our own original interpretations. The interpretation on which I focus calls attention to the symbolic value of the front and back wallpaper patterns, where "the 'front pattern' represents, among other things, the conventions that imprison [the narrator] [. . .] . The 'back' pattern will become the shape of a woman who crawls and shakes the bars of the front pattern, trying to get out" (Shumaker 90). The front wallpaper becomes symbolic of the patriarchal structures that surround the narrator. This wallpaper surrounds her in the same way patriarchal assumptions and oppression envelop the society that exists beyond the room in the ancestral home: "The narrator experiences her victimization as a conflict between her own personal feelings, perceived by feminist critics as healthy and positive, and the patriarchal society's view of what is proper behavior for women" (Kennard 76). From this perspective, the back pattern comes to represent her individual path toward liberation if only she could remove or alter the front pattern. Although not the only way to view the symbolically powerful wallpaper, these interpretations ask students to ponder important issues.

This method asks students to understand that multiple forces protect the male-dominated status quo and keep the front pattern and oppressive societal limitations in place. The relationship between the narrator and her husband provides a prime illustration. The narrator is a woman, wife, and patient being treated by John, a man, her husband, and doctor. Gender codes, marriage, and the medical profession all work to keep this woman in "her place." This threefold oppression magnifies the power of the front pattern of the wallpaper. While the narrator begins to grasp the problem of this system, the other feminine presence in the story re-inscribes the problem. The narrator writes of John's sister, Jennie: "She is a perfect and enthusiastic housekeeper, and hopes for no better profession. I verily believe she thinks it is the writing which made me sick" (33). Here I ask students to consider that Jennie may represent women who allow men to dominate their lives and society and wish for nothing more than to have and take care of children. I couple this interpretation with the possibility that postpartum depression may characterize the narrator as a societal outcast unable to fulfill the expected feminine functions in her society: raising children and housekeeping. Jennie happily fills in and will "do her duty." Later in the story when Jennie admits that she would like to tear down the wallpaper, our narrator notes, "How she betrayed herself that time!" (41). She has betrayed the male-dominated system to which she subscribes and thus her role in that structure. This sense of betrayal offers a focal point for this interpretation of the story.

I continue this method by asking students to discuss creeping in the context of the story. I find it important to work within the specific interpretation concerning the front and back wallpaper, while always staying open to the various ways that students view creeping or any aspect of the story. I make sure to keep room open for the reading I advance at first and the ones students possess. I foreground that, as the narrator describes the woman creeping in the back pattern, the reader is given access to another feminine figure other than Jennie. At first the woman in the back pattern must hide from patriarchy and creep at night only. Thus, the creeping potentially signifies a desire to remain hidden and work below the radar of the male-dominated world. However, as the story progresses, we see more creeping figures and ones willing to creep during the day and not just at night, including the narrator. Such figures may represent the growing tide of women who were unwilling to accept patriarchy as the only feasible system. Our narrator no longer can be viewed as an isolated figure but part of a larger movement to which students may feel joined. This movement involves challenging any system of oppression including gender and academic domination. The narrator and the other creeping women question the system that Jennie seems, on the surface, to accept. Gilman writes of the wallpaper, "I know a little of the principle of design, and I know this thing was not arranged on any laws of radiation, or alternation, or repetition, or symmetry, or anything else that I ever heard of" (34). However, she does more than allude to a lack of logic for the pattern; she questions why any sane person would accept the system. She notes, "On a pattern like this, by daylight, there is a lack of sequence, a defiance of law, that is a constant irritant to a normal mind" (37). These passages allow a reader to question if the narrator is either insane or a sane woman placed in an insane patriarchal system.

Determining the sanity of the patriarchal system rather than just the mental status of the narrator opens "The Yellow Wall-paper" to multiple readings based on the cultural situation and history of the reader. To tap into these personal histories, I assign journal writings. For Gilman's story, I give a journal assignment in two parts: the first part asks students to consider the possible symbolic value of the front and back wallpaper as a set-up for class discussion on that topic; the second part asks students if the narrator grows insane, is a sane person placed in an insane situation, or both. Students must bear in mind the ending and determine if the narrator finds liberation, desperate insanity, or possibly both. The journal questions ask students to mull over what other critics have examined for years. Critics question if the ending offers the narrator's triumph or defeat. Class discussion allows us to delve into what liberates or restricts the narrator because "the tension between the degree of her success or her failure, dramatically unresolved in the narrative, continues to be the dynamic propelling many of the new readings" (Hedges 230). This tension works well in the classroom setting as students work their way through important feminist issues.

The story does more than force us to question gender roles in our society but asks the following: does society have the ability to force us into certain lifestyles and modes of action based on gender, race, sexual preference, economic situation, age, or myriad other factors? If society does have that power, how does it manifest itself, and how do we resist or reinforce that control? How do we find and pull down the yellow wallpaper that surrounds us all? And what do we expose as our own back pattern? Teachers who effectively weave these questions into a discussion of "The Yellow Wall-paper" allow students to view their own lives through the lens of the story without ignoring crucial feminist readings of the text. Here students may build on what other critics have offered and retain originality. The discussion circles back to the students, and the process of reminding students that this approach merely represents one of many ways to read and question the story remains paramount. Teachers who stress reader response must not allow students to think that their readings are the only worthy ones and that all readings eventually come back to their own perceptions and history.

After working through reactions to the journal prompts, a follow-up question that invariably stimulates discussion asks students to consider if the situation of women has improved since the time of the story. Student responses usually affirm that progress has been made but that room for improvement exists. This question leads directly into a further examination of the differences between the front and back wallpaper. At this point I require students to offer their own original spin on what other critics have previously offered. Such a question prepares them for their research paper, stimulates discussion, and allows students to see how they can directly engage with other critics while still retaining their own voice. This step thwarts the interpretative bondage that stems from simply accepting symbolic interpretations of the story. To accomplish these goals, I ask students to ponder how they conform to, rebel against, or perpetuate gender codes in our society. I ask them to consider what wallpaper surrounds their own lives. It is vital for students to question the terms "male" and "female" and how we internalize their meanings. These prompts lead to an introduction about essentialism in literature and society. Gilman's story allows the class to question what being a specific gender or race means and how those ideas are culturally constructed and then perpetuated. I raise this conversation because it arises again when we discuss other literature by minority figures. Feminist scholars have grappled with the problems and power of essentialism when reading the story. The issue raises the question of whether or not the plight of one woman may represent the problems of an entire group of people or if the back pattern represents the "true self" of all women.[2] Of course any conception of a "true self" remains problematic, and a discussion of essentialism highlights these problems. It is a conversation that I stimulate early in the semester because, like reader response, it leads to complicated uncertainty that offers opportunities for expression rather than easy answers.

Issues of essentialism also invite comparisons between the narrator and her audience, regardless of gender, race, or economic status. The narrator of "The Yellow Wall-paper" has her husband/doctor and Jennie to advance stereotypical male/female roles, but in our culture the situation is more complicated. Students must wrestle with the influence of family, teachers, music, television, the Internet, advertising, dress codes, and a host of other forms that create their own yellow wallpaper. More importantly, students can realize that their own yellow wallpaper may try to dictate what it means to be more than just a man or a woman. Its influence may infiltrate countless aspects of their lives. Much like the narrator before her bout with depression, students often fail to realize the societal influences that help shape them, and they prefer to view themselves as autonomous individuals. Considering the common culture and language that surrounds us, such a notion of autonomy remains impossible. At best, we can only come to understand what forces shape us and how we react to those powers. By working through these issues early, I prepare students for later discussions concerning postmodern theory and literature that view the self as culturally constructed. I usually choose not to use words like postmodern or poststructural until later in the course, but some of the basic tenets of those terms come through when discussing Gilman's work.

In my class, we discuss the positives and negatives of essentialism, but the emphasis remains on awareness. I don't wish to force my students to think in a certain way, but I do want them to be informed about what surrounds them. However, asking the questions and pointing out these influences is not enough: "What students read matters as much as—if not more than—how they read [. . .]. A feminist approach to literary response must foreground the gender of the responders and must allow that classroom imbalances and hence conflicts are inevitable. We achieve community only by eliminating inequities. And inequities arise out of social and political factors that extend far beyond the classroom" (Flynn 82). Reader response must consider the gender of the responder, but this model also applies to different ethnicities, classes, and sexual orientations as well. Students must be aware not only of what affects their own lives but that others in the class have different influences and/or will respond differently to similar forces. If "ways of reading texts reflect ways of reading the world" (King and Morris 23), then the valuable feminist readings of the story bridge the gap to other approaches by showing the untenable nature of singular authoritative meanings when discussing either our society or the stories we read. Exclusively using a feminist reading of the text limits the reader just as the husband limits the narrator in the story. Although I find it inconceivable to teach this story without using feminist tools, I argue that those same tools allow us to move beyond feminist readings alone. While feminist readings remain intensely valuable, to discuss the story only in feminist terms restricts readers and places them in a form of interpretive bondage again. Asking students to determine their own yellow wallpaper allows them to explore feminism, patriarchy, and other forms of hegemonic rule. Students may create new conventions to discuss "The Yellow Wallpaper" in terms of race, class, sexuality, or any other cultural codes that they find working within and against them. Through the class, they examine a set of front and back wallpaper patterns based on their particular situation. Such a discussion asks students to introduce fresh and personal perspectives without ignoring the critical mass that exists concerning the story. In essence, it forces them to become their own critics and places their readings on the same level as the author, the critic, and the teacher. As with powerful feminist readings, these interpretations allow individuals to express their own cultural circumstances. They also make other members of the class aware of the different situations that exist within the classroom community. These readings of Gilman's work allow us (and I absolutely include the teacher in that learning process) to learn from each other.

The journals invariably describe the text as frustrating, difficult, and compelling. I have read a wide range of symbolic features of the front and back wallpaper; however, most students view the front wallpaper as sign of growing insanity, depression, loneliness, lack of creativity, and freedom, and they see the back as a respite from these intolerable measures. I collect their journal assignments before we discuss the story in class; I find that, prior to our discussion, rarely do students make connections between the wallpaper and their own lives, although some do see the gender issues that I use to start our class discussion. One important follow-up assignment asks students to discuss, in small groups, my question about what cultural wallpaper surrounds them, what traditions or rituals they simply accept without questioning, and how they react to those influences. For these questions, I find that smaller groups generally stimulate better responses and lead to an excellent discussion when we discuss what their specific groups found. Sometimes I assign another journal writing entry, asking students to pick out and discuss the influences that surround them after spending a few days actually focusing on them, especially advertising and the media. What students identify as the wallpaper that encircles them is always unpredictable, and that fact keeps me teaching the same story each semester. Students make connections between their family, their religion, their race, gender, sexuality, what it means to be a student, and often come in contact with others who hold extremely different views. Many students have a working understanding of their own influences (though not always), but equally as many seem to lack that understanding about what forces help create other individuals in the class. Exposing this establishes a dialogue that continues throughout the semester, and large segments of my class learn a lot about themselves and others through this one story. Of course not all students suddenly become receptive to this community exchange, and many do not develop great insights about the culture that surrounds them because of their reading of "The Yellow Wallpaper." However, they can no longer ignore the issues, and I use the rest of the semester to build on this invaluable opening lesson.

The most obvious manifestation of my pedagogical approach to "The Yellow Wall-paper" remains my students' research paper assignment. I wish to provide one specific example where this approach produced an interesting and excellent paper about Gilman's work. A student named Jocelyn e-mailed me about her growing concern with the research paper requirement in our class. My expectation that students will strive for original interpretations revolving around the concept of intertextuality (where a "text" is not limited to works read in class but includes myriad cultural structures as well) often poses problems. Students each do a presentation in class to start their research, but they are not forced to write their paper on the same story on which they present. Jocelyn wrote the following message:

> I did my presentation on the "The Yellow Wall-paper" and it's one of my favorite short stories, but the problem is that all angles that the story has been examined through have been completely exhausted. I don't know how I am going to get an interesting paper out of it, especially one that is 8–10 pages long.

This e-mail surprised me because Jocelyn is both a bright student and one of the few English majors in that class. She had fallen into the trap of thinking that every approach to this story had already been used. During her presentation she had examined the important feminist issues of the text and had an excellent understanding of Gilman's work. However, she didn't feel that she had anything original to add. I included the following questions in my e-mailed response:

1) Why does "The Yellow Wall-paper" interest you?
2) What other things in our society relate to what interests you about "The Yellow Wall-paper" (other texts, films, cultural institutions, and movements) and represent something about which you'd like to learn more?
3) Consider analyzing "The Yellow Wall-paper" through the intertextual relationship with the answer to question 2.

Eventually Jocelyn found that the oppressive atmosphere presented in the story intrigued her the most, and she coupled this with a recent environmental concern. She expanded on Tom Lutz's study of "The Yellow Wall-paper," in *American Nervousness, 1903: An Anecdotal History*, where he discusses the medical effects of using arsenic in wallpaper paint and Gilman's story. Jocelyn opted to show the similarities between the narrator's struggles and our own quest for environmental freedom from corporate and business entities that try to hide the pollution and damage that they create. The paper offered an excellent forum for Jocelyn to compare the individual oppression of the narrator with wider systemic oppressive forces still evident in our society. More importantly, Jocelyn educated herself about a story she enjoyed and an environmental concern about which she cared deeply. The paper became a chance to learn something that interested her rather than an attempt to try and provide what she thought her teacher would want. Although this approach works for any paper, I want to stress that it starts with the critical freedom introduced early in the semester with "The Yellow Wall-paper."

This approach to Gilman's text challenges Hirsch's problems with authority and indeterminacy. I encourage students to formulate their own opinions and respectfully critique the interpretations of others, including my own. For midterms and finals, students are expected to have an understanding of the interpretations that I present and to use critical thinking skills to develop their own readings. Often the best students in my class excel because they disagree with a presented reading and formulate their own opinion. I retain the needed authority to organize and run a class, but I quickly diffuse that power when it comes to interpreting stories. Students are graded not on whether I agree with them but how well they can argue their own points. It isn't enough to be original or just have an understanding of the readings of others: students must do both in order to become their own critics and to perform well.

When students strip away the oppressive authority of the author, critic, and teacher, they act in the same capacity as the narrator as she tears down the wallpaper. Giving students equal access to a text encourages them to invest more time in reading the story for their own interpretations rather than trying to determine the "correct" reading. The teacher must make sure that students understand the value of authorial intentions and published critical opinions but not at the expense of their own ideas. Students then realize that their own critiques are one of many plausible interpretations. Thus, they must respect the ideas of others just as they expect that same consideration. Gilman's "The Yellow Wall-paper" helps introduce and establish this productive community, especially for scholars teaching students in mandatory introductory literature classes who have little experience with literary theory.

Notes

1. See Elaine R. Hedges, "'Out at Last'? 'The Yellow Wallpaper' after Two Decades of Feminist Criticism." This article traces feminist readings of the story since her "Afterword" for the 1973 Feminist Press edition. The essay offers one of the finest starting points for teachers and scholars because it shows the evolution of feminist approaches to the text, including important points of disagreement.
2. See Susan S. Lanser, "Feminist Criticism, 'The Yellow Wallpaper,' and the Politics of Color in America." Lanser argues that establishing a feminist identity for women as a group runs the risk of creating another oppressive label, one using the same tools as men who impose their version of womanhood on others. In the final paragraph of her article "Out at Last?," Elaine R. Hedges also discusses the problems of identity politics in the story. While Hedges understands that determining a core identity for women is problematic, she believes not recognizing one depoliticizes the story. For her, the essential identity lies in the subordinate status of women. The issue is important to establish because it is one that students often fail to consider.

Works Cited

Bauer, Dale. "Introduction: Cultural and Historical Background." *The Yellow Wallpaper.* Ed. Dale Bauer. Boston and New York: Bedford Books, 1998. 3–28.

Bleich, David. "Reading from Inside and Outside One's Community." *Practicing Theory in Introductory College Literature Courses*. Eds. James M. Cahalan and David B. Downing. Urbana, IL: NCTE, 1991. 19–35.

Buckler, Patricia Prandini. "Combining Personal and Textual Experience: A Reader-Response Approach to Teaching American Literature." *Practicing Theory in Introduc-*

tory College Literature Courses. Eds. James M. Cahalan and David B. Downing. Urbana, IL: NCTE, 1991. 36–46.

Dock, Julie Bates, Comp. and Ed. *Charlotte Perkins Gilman's "The Yellow Wall-paper" and the History of Its Publication and Reception: A Critical Edition and Documentary Casebook*. University Park, PA: The Pennsylvania State University Press, 1998.

Flynn, Elizabeth A. "Engendering the Teaching of Reading." *College Literature* 18(2): (June 1991): 80–93.

Freire, Paulo. *Pedagogy of the Oppressed*. 1970. New York: Continuum, 1990.

Gilman, Charlotte Perkins. "The Yellow Wallpaper." 1892. *Charlotte Perkins Gilman's "The Yellow Wall-paper and the History of Its Publication and Reception: A Critical Edition and Documentary Casebook*. Comp. and Ed. Julie Bates Dock. University Park, PA: The Pennsylvania State University Press, 1998. 29–42.

Hedges, Elaine R. "'Out at Last'? 'The Yellow Wallpaper' after Two Decades of Feminist Criticism." *Critical Essays on Charlotte Perkins Gilman*. Ed. Joanne B. Karpinski. New York: G.K. Hall & Co, 1992. 222–233.

Hirsch Jr., E. D. "In Defense of the Author." *Intention and Interpretation*. Ed. Gary Iseminger. Philadelphia: Temple University Press, 1992. 11–23.

Kennard, Jean E. "Convention Coverage or How to Read Your Own Life." *New Literary History* 8.1 (Autumn 1981): 69–88.

King, Jeannette, and Pam Morris. "On Not Reading Between the Lines: Modes of Reading in 'The Yellow Wallpaper." *Studies in Short Fiction* 26.1 (Winter 1989): 23–32.

Lanser, Susan S. "Feminist Criticism, 'The Yellow Wallpaper,' and the Politics of Color in America." *Feminist Studies* 15.3 (Fall 1989): 415–41.

Lutz, Tom. *American Nervousness, 1903: An Anecdotal History*. Ithaca: Cornell University Press, 1991.

Mailloux, Steven. "The Turns of Reader-Response Criticism." *Conversations: Contemporary Critical Theory and the Teaching of Literature*. Eds. Charles Moran and Elizabeth Penfield. Urbana, IL: NCTE, 1990. 38–54.

Shumaker, Conrad. "Realism, Reform, and the Audience: Charlotte Perkins Gilman's Unreadable Wallpaper." *Arizona Quarterly* 47.1 (Spring 1991): 81–93.

Wimsatt, W. K., and Monroe C. Beardsley. "The Intentional Fallacy," *The Critical Tradition: Classic Texts and Contemporary Trends*. Ed. David H. Richter. 2nd ed. Boston: Bedford Books, 1998.

Janet Gebhart Auten

HELPING STUDENTS DECODE THE DIFFICULT TEXT

"The Yellow Wall-paper" and the Sequential Response

Charlotte Perkins Gilman's style and subject matter have made "The Yellow Wall-paper" a rich teaching text as demonstrated by the essays in this collection. One of its attractions is its allegorical picture of the act of reading, with the opportunity it offers to help students become more aware of their own ways of reading and writing. By now a familiar staple of literature, gender studies, American history, and many social science courses, Gilman's story of the woman fascinated by patterns in the paper both describes and demands critical reading. And it not only embodies the effort to read any difficult and disturbing text but also posits writing as an important means of coming to terms with such difficulty: denied her writing outlet, the narrator gets literally lost in her "reading." It seems particularly fitting, then, to ask students to use the lifeline that the narrator was denied: to write their way out of the difficulty of reading this story. But prompting and supporting such writing present a challenge to teachers. The following discussion describes the process of developing such an assignment as a way to consider the complex demands this text makes on students and on teachers. Over several semesters of working with student responses to "The Yellow Wall-paper," I found the writing assignment needed to help students respond to the text while counteracting their tendency to read too quickly, to get derailed by detail, or to rely too easily on a single, convenient interpretive lens.

"The Yellow Wall-paper" asks readers to weigh evidence, to be discerning, and to "read between the lines" much as Gilman's narrator "reads" the wallpaper until she gradually perceives patterns of meaning in it. But just as the narrator struggles to figure out the complex pattern of her tattered wallpaper, many students find a first reading of the story dauntingly difficult. In eight semesters of working with this text in undergraduate women's and gender studies classes, I have found that, like the narrator, students can get lost in their reading of the story in various ways. [1] Many students seem to find the story either pointless and "boring" or inordinately upsetting and disorienting. Of course, unlike the narrator, students struggling with "The Yellow Wall-paper" can simply stop reading. But the narrator's process of discovery suggests that even reluctant readers may be drawn into the process of puzzling out its patterns of meaning *if* they can slow their reading pace and heighten their awareness of the effect the text has on them. My aim was to encourage students to get beyond their tendency to dismiss the story as "too confusing," "too weird," or "too boring" by replicating the narrator's step-by-step *process* of sense making in a journal-writing assignment. In her exploration of the wallpaper, the narrator not only reads visual cues but also gradually invests the wallpaper with personal significance, *watching* it by the hour with all of her senses engaged. But while we might hope students would "watch" their reading carefully as well, one week with "Wall-paper" doesn't offer students time to invest themselves in reading as the narrator does. A reading response assignment can encourage students to "watch" carefully, engage their personal experiences and their senses, and try to see what is going on behind the surface pattern of the story.

Initial Encounters

When we started to develop this approach, my teaching partner and I had been working with weekly response journal assignments for our women's and gender studies class that drew a diverse group of 60 students from all levels and disciplines at our private, medium-size university. We asked students to record their emotional responses to each week's reading assignments, to try to connect what they read to their own experience, and then to discuss their readings in terms of course themes. We consciously modeled this method for our course on feminist ideas about reading, which posits interpretation as constructed within a context of feeling as well as analysis, personal as well as textual experience, political as well as literary resonance.[2] However, these weekly assignments asked students to read and then write responses after reading in the conventional way. For the "Wall-paper" assignment, I altered the approach, directing students to keep a running account of their reactions *while reading*, much as Gilman's narrator provides a running commentary on her impressions of the wallpaper as she looks at it. Rather than using the words, "tell what happens" that simply start students narrating, the assignment directed them to "tell what happens to *you.*" Students were told to "record your progress through the text, pausing every few paragraphs as you read to write about the feelings and ideas that come to you," producing what I call the sequential-response journal.

This simple directive worked well to evoke students' initial impressions, which are much like the narrator's own. Arriving at the old country estate, Gilman's narrator notes "there is something strange about the house—I can feel it" (30). Students frequently record a similar reaction to the early part of the story. As one put it, "*It makes me feel as if there is something shady or not right with her husband.*"

The narrator's initial reaction to the paper in the bedroom at the top of the house is a dismissive but dramatic judgment:

> I never saw a worse paper in my life.
>
> One of those sprawling, flamboyant patterns committing every artistic sin. It is dull enough to confuse the eye in following, pronounced enough to constantly irritate and provoke study, and when you follow the lame uncertain curves for a little distance they suddenly commit suicide—plunge off at outrageous angles, destroy themselves in unheard of contradictions. (31)

Like the narrator's first evaluation of the wallpaper, students' initial responses often come to a quick judgement as did the student entry that pronounced "*their relationship most odd. One usually is closest emotionally to her husband and family, yet these are the people whom the woman feels most alienated from. . . . I do not expect that from my marriage when I get married. . . .*"

Few contemporary college students will, at the outset, identify with a nineteenth-century woman who finds herself trapped in an odd room at the top of a big old house in the country, and their responses often reflect impatience or outrage with the "lame uncertain curves" of her acquiescence to her husband's orders. As one student put it, "*I found myself, at the beginning, getting angry with [her] passiveness.*"

However, as Judith Fetterley has pointed out, the "unheard of contradictions" at the heart of the story involve more than marital friction. At stake are conflicting definitions of sanity and reality. The narrator attempts at first to go along with her husband's definitions, what Fetterley calls "John's Text," while maintaining her own view—trying to write on her own. Questions emerge in students' journals as the narrator herself begins to wonder about agency. She confesses, "Personally, I believe that congenial work, with excitement and change, would do me good. But what is one to do?" (30). We often see the question posed by one student as, "*why is it always 'John says'? Why can't she say things herself?*"

But students' impatience often gives way as the narrator further describes the unbridgeable gulf between her husband—who "has no patience with faith, an intense horror of superstition, and [. . .] scoffs openly at any talk of things not to be felt and seen and put down in figures" (Gilman 29)—and herself, who possesses an imagination which in her childhood could provide "more entertainment and terror out of blank walls and plain furniture than most children could find in a toy-store" (32). This moment in the narrative seems to invite readers to recall their own childhood imaginative experiences, especially nighttime imaginings, and it also evokes sympathy for the narrator from those students who see John as a disapproving father figure.

Having already become accustomed to attending to the personal in previous weeks' journal assignments, students often connect this passage to their own childhood fantasies. One example shows a student suddenly finding a way into the story through such a personal connection:

> *when I started reading it I thought they must be kidding; this is pretty boring. [But] when she started talking about the wallpaper (which I knew had to have some importance because of the title) all I could think about was the objects that I see in the wood paneling that I have in my house in the basement. One day I notice a rooster and a person's head in the wood pattern no one else can see and think I am crazy but I know they are there. . . . The patterns in the paneling I see don't move though. Then I started to feel sorry for her because she wanted to leave knowing that her condition was going to worsen because of the wallpaper.*

It is significant that the transformation of the narrator and these student readers takes place as imagination comes into play. When students begin to sympathize through shared experience, a more probing and personal kind of reading becomes possible.

Although asking students simply to record their feelings as they read worked to slow their reading and helped them wrestle with the text more carefully, their entries sometimes became catalogues of responses such as this list of feelings:

> *I felt excited on page 34 when she begins to fall in love with the wallpaper. I'm angry on page 39 because John doesn't want her to take care of herself for her own sake only for his. . . . I feel hope on page 43 when she discovers that the pattern does move. I find it exciting*

> *that the woman behind is shaking it. I find myself hoping that all hidden women will shake things up.*

While this reading log helped the student find the feminist message about "hidden women" in the story, a response journal also should steer students toward an awareness of how and why their feelings shape their reading, going beyond a simple summary of their reactions.

Moreover, simply directing students to write in stages and establishing a practice of personal writing about reading did not address the particular disorienting impact of this tale on its readers. Just as Gilman situates her subject in a remote room where she must make sense of her surroundings, she positions her readers in a similar situation. While the narrator sees in the room's ugly yellow wallpaper "a lack of sequence, a defiance of law, that is a constant irritant to a normal mind" (37), the reader may experience a similarly irritating "lack of sequence" in the increasingly obsessive narration. We found in reading our students' response journals for the "Yellow Wall-paper" assignment that recording reactions as they read only gave some readers a space to scribble out their confusion and/or irritation. The job of the sequential response journal was to help students notice and even *value* that irritation and other feelings about the narrative and make them productive parts of student readings. But the assignment did not prompt readers' reflection on their responses. As the narrator reads more deeply into the wallpaper and students progress further into the story, we saw the response journals document difficulties and defeats for readers as they tried to figure out the intense interior monologue of this narrator in her "nervous condition."

The narrator tells us that John has warned her: "I must use my will and self-control and not let any silly fancies run away with me" (35), but after two weeks, she has begun attaching emotional response to her reading of the wallpaper, confessing, "I get positively angry with the impertinence of it and the everlastingness. Up and down and sideways they crawl, and those absurd, unblinking eyes are everywhere" (32). Similarly, students seemed to get caught in the story's well-known whirlpool of feelings. One student, for example, found herself "*haunted about her obsession with not liking the wallpaper. . . mad that he won't let her write! I think he is her problem. . . . I feel, like I'm going crazy reading about her fascination with the wallpaper.*" Many students similarly seemed to plunge into the story only to be either lost or alienated by its emotional extremes. It was apparent that the sequential response journal assignment needed to function somehow as "will and self-control" to help students find a workable reading position somewhere between the extremes of "drowning" and detachment. By simply asking students to record their impressions of the story as they read, we offered a useful strategy for going about reading. But for many students, following this directive alone seemed to reinforce reading pitfalls.

Extremes of Reading

The problems student readers face as they wrestle with difficult reading are illuminated by Elizabeth Flynn's analysis of the patterns of resistance and engagement in college students' responses to literature. With the assumption that "reading involves a confrontation between self and 'other'" (267), Flynn describes students' reading in terms of submission, dominance, or interaction with text. At one extreme, readers may empathize with the story to such a degree that they lose their balance as do students who identify so closely with the narrator of "The Yellow Wall-paper" that they become entrapped in a shifting, unstable subjectivity. Flynn found that this was a common response to complex texts among first-year college student readers, who may become anxiously "entangled in the events" of the story. As one of our students wrote out of such entanglement, "*The narrator seemed to successfully pull me down with her. As she sunk into the hole created by the people who were supposed to help her, I found myself slipping right beside her.*" Another wrote, "*As the story continued, and I suppose the wife's mental state gets worse, I felt confused and trapped. . . . I cannot comprehend the images that went through the wife's head. She speaks crazily.*" Here, as Flynn puts it, "the text overpowers the reader and so eliminates the reader's powers of discernment" (268). Of course, this also describes Gilman's narrator, who confides, "You think you have mastered it, but just as you get well underway in following, it turns a back-somersault and there you are. It slaps you in the face, knocks you down, and tramples upon you. It is like a bad dream" (37).

Submissive readers, like the narrator herself, face a losing battle to stay removed enough from the narrative to discern patterns of meaning in an alien environment. In our first efforts to assign a response journal, we saw many disturbing instances of submissive reading such as that of the student who reported, "*I found myself scared whenever the mention of the wallpaper occurred. . . . One day John's wife sees the wallpaper move. I got frightened because it took me by surprise.*" We quickly realized that the assignment had to work to counteract such over-identification. Just as the narrator notes "The color is hideous enough, and infuriating enough, but the pattern is torturing" (37), too many of our students found themselves "*Tortured as she describes the eyesore wallpaper*" and unable to come to any understanding of the story. Therefore, we began to construct a more directive journal prompt, one that would create a context for reading. While the idea of letting students come to the story unaware of

Gilman's personal experience and purposes in writing had seemed interesting to *us*, some of our unsuspecting students clearly needed to be bolstered with historical perspective in order to be able to find a foothold in the story. In subsequent semesters, we made sure to "set the stage" for students' reading, including how and why this is a "difficult text." To the original assignment, we added: "Note especially any passages which affect you strongly or which connect in some way to your own experience. Why do they affect you or connect to you particularly?"

At the other extreme of Flynn's scale of response are the readers who "dominate" a text as John dominates his wife. These readers so thoroughly resist the text that they evade subjective response entirely, remaining detached and "objective." Such students often continue to express exasperation with the story throughout their journals and, like John, fail to comprehend the narrator's viewpoint at all. One student grumbled, "*I am starting to think she really is crazy after she keeps on talking about that stupid wallpaper. What is the point?*" Another echoed John's diagnosis in writing that "*people can become so wrapped up in their imagination that they lose all sense of real and unreal.*" It is precisely this rationalist dichotomy between "real" and "imagined" which underlies John's view—and that of many student readers. Most students have been schooled to try to read "objectively" and to link objectivity with the "real" and subjectivity with "imagination"—just as the narrator's solicitous and patronizing husband does in the story.

Unlike their submissive counterparts, who become enmeshed in the shifts and inconsistencies of the narrative, dominating readers see contradictions simply as textual problems. For example, one student asked, "*Would a normal person stare at walls all day and night long? This is the great contradiction in this story. We are to see her as normal and know that she isn't at the same time.*" Such a reader can easily dismiss the narrator—and her narrative—much as John "comforts" his wife by belittling her pain. Other students hold the text at a distance through standard literary analysis. For example, one student neatly subverted the purpose of the reading record by focusing her attention on style, commenting, "*The first thing I noticed about this story is the writing style. It is written in journal entry style which I find very intriguing.*" Another student suggested that the narrator's situation comes not from psychological or social forces but fits into the familiar genre of supernatural horror: "*The paper really did drive her insane.*"

Just as John maintains his distance by regarding his wife as a medical "case," students may also write their way out of the story by taking the diagnostic stance such as, "*I tend to believe the husband more than the wife. . . . I get the impression that she is really sick, but it seems entirely mental. When she talks about always being "nervous" it gives me the impression of someone who is schizophrenic. . . . I really believe she has gone crazy.*"

Another common diagnosis we found in journals focuses on the narrator's symptoms of postpartum depression. As one reader put it, "*I think that the wife simply suffered from the disorder that happens after a woman gives birth. . . . Because I am not married and do not have any children, I cannot relate to this story.*" Such refusal to engage with the text seemed to be a lazy way out—but it also might mask anxiety about the story such as this: "*I found it especially difficult to read TYW because it was such a traumatic story. Not only is a woman forced to deal with the hormonal changes following pregnancy but also with the male domination that convinces her she is suffering from hysterical anxiety.*" Here the adolescent tendency to be judgmental can feed into "response" as well. At the extreme, students evade the story altogether with journal entries like this: "*She is being redundant, and is just babbling with a pen,*" a conclusion with interesting overtones of the reductive attitude of husband toward wife in Gilman's story.

Such entries raise a key issue in assigning personal response writing: we have students who for various reasons see the story as threatening. Perhaps they fear they will become submissive readers and so choose to keep the text at arm's length rather than risk submersion in it. Whatever the reason, the assignment needed to incorporate a way of disarming the threat of self-disclosure while providing a place to explore the strong feelings that the story evokes. The two extremes of reading, whether a too sympathetic or too analytic approach, made preparation and direction important for our revised assignment. But we realized that a third element for the "Yellow Wall-paper" assignment was reflection. For the following semester's assignment, we added a sentence that asked students to "Look back at your responses. How and why did this story affect you? How did your feelings and your attitude change as you read through the story?"

Working Toward a Balance

In creating a better journal assignment, we were guided by responses from our students who seemed to be able to integrate their empathetic and their analytic responses. Such students, who neither impose convenient conventions on the story nor let the story overwhelm them, belong to Flynn's third category of readers, those who seem to "create a kind of dialogue" (Flynn 268) between themselves and the text. For our revised sequential response journal assignment, we looked for ways to evoke such a dialogue: neither submissive nor dominating, neither lost in nor shut out of the text. We realized possibilities for the assignment as we saw some students thoughtfully map their progressive involvement in the story:

> *As I continue to read I am getting feelings of uneasiness: 'The color is hideous enough. . . .' I feel very unsettled, but my analytical side is beginning to show. I am wondering what that wallpaper is to her. Why does it have such an effect on her, after all no matter how ugly it may be, it is only wallpaper? I have suspicions that she is seeing her reflection in it.*
>
> *Yes! I was right: 'now I am quite sure that it is a woman.'*

This student's gradual gleaning of insight through recording responses showed that the sequential response could help readers write their way through "The Yellow Wall-paper." While they did not necessarily report profound truths or startling discoveries, some students seemed to use the writing productively to reposition themselves from outside the material to "inside," from passive observer to active participant.

After considering the responses our students wrote, we saw our assignment goals as threefold: it needed to (1) create a context for reading and writing, making the how and why of the assignment explicit, and while we could (2) build on our established practice of response writing, which values the personal as much as the analytical, we also needed to (3) offer a framework for reflection and analysis. Looking to some of the more balanced and reflective responses from our students, we identified three characteristics that marked most student readings of the difficult text: self-awareness, personal connection, and analytical perspective.

One characteristic of more balanced readings was that students were able to put themselves into the story but keep out of the submissive trap by monitoring their own reactions:

> *By the end of the story I could feel my muscles tightening and I felt tense, almost helpless. . . . The wife becomes completely absorbed in the wallpaper and it controls her mind. . . . It teases and taunts her. . . . I just wish I could help her and fix what it is that is wrong with her mind.*

Other students replicated and reflected on the narrator's anxiety and unhappiness but also tried to pinpoint the source of their response. One student wrote, for example,

> *I find that as I read, I begin to share the narrator's bitterness and pain. . . . Her writing and description of the wallpaper alludes to several vivid images of death. I was shaken by this imagery ("suddenly commit suicide"), her wording so precisely chosen to describe simple patterns in wallpaper.*

These students apparently understood the point of their writing assignment: to *notice* their own reading and the way the story shapes it. In order to clarify the assignment, we needed to explain this more clearly, to give students a better idea of their *purpose* in writing and to support a self-reflexive sense of *what* they were writing.

The balanced discussions we admired most were not only suffused with self-awareness but also enriched with some personal dimension. A second characteristic of the effective discussions was their ability to employ personal experience as a lens through which to read the text. The weekly response writing in our course is predicated on a feminist view of texts as always both personal and political, and we ask students to mine their own life experiences as well as previous reading experiences in responding to texts. In writing about a personal connection to the story, students add a "real" dimension to reading, especially those to whom the nineteenth-century tale seems otherwise a remote fantasy. As the narrator of "The Yellow Wall-paper" shares her ambivalent attempts to assert her own subjectivity in a world which privileges a different (male) subject and, failing in that, to "read" the complex pattern of her bedroom wallpaper, students may put themselves in the narrator's place as frustrated outsiders in the academy. Students who have struggled with reading made personal connections even as they struggled to follow the threads of her meandering monologue. As one student wrote,

> *I had a very hard time reading TYW. I had to read it over 3 times before I felt I understood it and even then I did not fully grasp all of it. I felt very connected to Gilman when she was having difficulty writing. As a student who is learning disabled, I have spent my life struggling with and hating school, especially writing.*

This reader has not only conflated Gilman and her narrator but also has transformed the narrator's efforts to assert her own voice into an internal battle that mirrors her own struggles in school. Our task was to help such students think about the parallels to personal experience as a path to greater understanding of the text. Most students are familiar with the standard search for something "relevant to your life" in reading for school assignments, a task that can lure readers into submission or solipsism. The journal assignment must steer students away from such pitfalls by prompting them to use their experience as a tool—a way to see "inside" the story.

In one student's narration of her reading, we saw the kind of response we were looking for, one in which students come to terms with the text through a personal connection:

> *Like the narrator I, too, was forced to endure a similar atmosphere at home. I felt as though I had to also be alone because I hated living under the same roof with my two parents. It was to the point where I was always physically ill as a result of my home situation. I had constant headaches and stomach problems as a result of nerves. Going away to college was my way of tearing down the wallpaper in that room. . . . [the narrator] had to*

> *uproot all the feelings and long hours that she had spent in the room. She had to free herself from the confinement of the room and her thoughts that were placed and hidden in the wallpaper. I feel closer to the narrator for I see so much of myself in her. We both tore down our wallpapers as a means of escape.*

The narrator's increasingly unstable outlook, which creates anxiety in "submissive" readers, provokes this student's efforts to read the "Wall-paper" through the lens of her own experience. Not only did her self-awareness allow her to empathize with the narrator while still maintaining her separate identity as a reader, but also she was able to use her personal connection to find wonderful insight, reading both the story and herself in fresh ways.

The response journal assignment seeks to enable students to achieve such a reading by drawing on both emotional and intellectual responses. A student may write, "*Who is this woman? It's disturbing and makes me think we've lost the narrator completely to insanity. I want to save her!*" with a clear sense of engagement that seems to avoid the pitfalls of excessive anxiety or detachment. She finds the story "disturbing" but comments on the narrator's apparent "insanity" from the perspective of a concerned observer.

A third characteristic we wanted to evoke in the journals was this kind of reflective awareness, a sense of what happened to them as readers. As they progress through "The Yellow Wall-paper," all readers must negotiate their position with a sometimes-overpowering text. If, as Flynn defines it, the reading process involves the merging of reader and text "so self and other coexist" (268), then the reader's problem in reading "The Yellow Wall-paper" becomes clear: Gilman asks the reader to "coexist" with an apparently hysterical subject, a narrator on the edge of sanity. As they narrated their reading experiences, some students showed us that they could make this difficult negotiation by translating the terms of the story into images, by literally *figuring it out*.

As the narrator begins to discern her own intersection with the wallpaper, remarking "I didn't realize for a long time what the thing was that showed behind, that dim sub-pattern, but now I am quite sure it is a woman" (42), one student saw that the wallpaper represented the narrator herself when, "*She describes how the wall paper seems to permeate through the house. As I read this I get the feeling that she means her illness is beginning to go everywhere she does. She can no longer escape herself.*" Another student noted the way "*She and this paper intersect and wrap around one another.*" The process of decoding this difficult text seemed similarly to involve an intersection of readers and their reading, which depended on readers' willingness to simultaneously see things from the narrator's perspective but also read the wallpaper for themselves.

Another student showed us the profound possibilities in using both the personal connection as a lens through which to make sense of the story and monitoring her own response as reader:

> *I know how that feels, that feeling of needing to stifle my thoughts and/or emotions for the benefit of others. When she thinks about the horrid color and the smell, it reminds me of the way that women are taught to think about their bodies. She makes reference to this tainted wallpaper ("smoldering unclean yellow"), and I feel that it reflects how she feels about herself and her sexuality.*

Here the student shows the kind of double vision that allows readers to negotiate the story successfully.

A Context for Reading

With these types of responses in mind, we revised our assignment to make its purpose explicit and set a clear context for writing. We introduced the writing assignment as a kind of dialogue between reader and text in which students should strive for a balance between empathy and judgment, involvement and detachment. The journal entries of student readers who were able to strike such a balance and come to terms with this difficult text suggested how we might add to our original, one-sentence assignment. The revised journal assignment asks students to

1. Read the story, stopping frequently to jot down their feelings and thoughts
2. Note any particular passages which affect them strongly and/or connect to their own experience in some way
3. Think about how and why they are affected and how and why their feelings change as they read.

After writing their records of reading, students come to class ready for small-group sharing of ideas and interpretations. In class, we extend that process through group discussions and ask each group to share its findings with us all at the end of the class session, to create a kind of group "reading" of the text. As students map their progress and process of reading the story and then later create collective, multivocal readings in class, they can begin to develop a more sophisticated sense of critical reading as well as a more complex appreciation of the story the "Wall-paper" has to tell.

In an academic setting, where reading is often seen as a way of acquiring information, students may interpret a reader-response assignment as a weird new way of asking them to explain what the story "is about" or simply another way of asking them whether they "liked it" or not. Nancy Comley argues that since "students almost always read for someone else [. . .] in a power hierarchy in which the teacher is the 'holder of the real meaning' of a literary text as well as the dispenser of grades," students tend to stay "outside the text" (180). Comley suggests that the teaching of reading and writing should be directed toward creating an awareness of the experiences which influence the reader and the "positions from which we read" (190–91). "The Yellow Wall-paper" is a text that can teach us how to do that.

Just as the narrator of "The Yellow Wall-paper" gradually discovers patterns of meaning in the wallpaper, student readers somehow will find their way through the text. But the sequential response journal assignment seeks to engage students in tracking their own process of sense-making and to make them more conscious and deliberate in their effort at the construction of meaning. That experience, in turn, can help them negotiate other challenging texts without either staying outside or becoming immersed in their reading. The payoff in assigning a sequential response journal is not only that student readers may become both more affectively and more effectively engaged with "The Yellow Wall-paper," but also that they may become better readers. By writing their way through "The Yellow Wall-paper," students can develop a deeper understanding of the complex factors that affect their reading and emerge better equipped to tackle other difficult texts.

Notes

1. I have been privileged to share the teaching of this interdisciplinary course, "Women's Voices Through Time," with Professor Valerie French of the history department. The pedagogical practices described in this article are the result of our collaborative work and of the valuable responses we have received from students.
2. See Flynn and Schweickart, eds. *Gender and Reading*.

Works Cited

Comley, Nancy R. "Reading and Writing Genders." *Reorientations: Critical Theories and Pedagogies*. Eds. Bruce Henricksen and Thais E. Morgan. Urbana: University of Illinois Press, 1990. 179–192.

Dock, Julie Bates, Comp. and Ed. *Charlotte Perkins Gilman's "The Yellow Wall-paper" and the History of Its Publication and Reception: A Critical Edition and Documentary Casebook*. University Park, PA: The Pennsylvania State University Press, 1998.

Fetterley, Judith. "Reading about Reading: 'A Jury of Her Peers,' 'The Murders in the Rue Morgue,' and 'The Yellow Wallpaper.'" *Gender and Reading: Essays on Readers,*

Texts, and Contexts. Eds. Elizabeth A. Flynn and Patrocinio P. Schweickart. Baltimore: Johns Hopkins University Press, 1986. 147–164.

Flynn, Elizabeth A. "Gender and Reading." *Gender and Reading: Essays on Readers, Texts, and Contexts*. Ed. Elizabeth A. Flynn and Patrocinio P. Schweickart. Baltimore: Johns Hopkins University Press, 1986. 267–88.

Gilman, Charlotte Perkins. "The Yellow Wallpaper." 1892. *Charlotte Perkins Gilman's "The Yellow Wall-paper and the History of Its Publication and Reception: A Critical Edition and Documentary Casebook*. Comp. and Ed. Julie Bates Dock. University Park, PA: The Pennsylvania State University Press, 1998. 29–42.

Gina Wisker

BREAKDOWN, BREAKTHROUGH, OR BRAINWASH?

A Dialogic Approach to Charlotte Perkins Gilman's "The Yellow Wall-paper"

This essay developed out of the experience of reading and teaching Gilman's text with two groups of students. The first was a group of third-year undergraduates, many of them mature women students, some of whom had experienced, nursed, and treated breakdown and depression. The second was a University Continuing Education group, several members of which had suffered from depression, and two of whom are family therapists. Teaching this text to these two groups caused me to realize that readings of "The Yellow Wall-paper," such as those of Gilbert and Gubar, Kennard, MacPike, and Schöpp-Schilling, that privilege mental breakdown as a form of "breakthrough" can present difficulties for students with backgrounds in health care or mental illness. This essay does not propose that the "breakdown equals breakthrough" reading needs to be eliminated. However, it does argue that Gilman's text needs to be read and taught in a "dialogic" way that holds different readings in productive tension and validates students' responses.

"The Yellow Wall-paper" has become a feminist classic largely because of its potential to be read as exploring mental breakdown as a response to late- and post-Victorian middle-class women's repression and incarceration in their roles as "angel in the parlor." In charting the increasing breakdown of a middle-class woman who may be suffering postpartum depression and who is confined—or who confines herself—to an attic nursery bedroom, the text exposes the destructive equation of resistance to these roles with hysteria. The narrator's madness at the end of "The Yellow Wall-paper" therefore critiques the oppression and silencing of women. In a patriarchal system that prevents her from expressing herself and realizing her potential, her breakdown is really a response to the madness of gender oppression.

This "breakdown equals breakthrough" reading has also been applied to other women's texts chronicling mental illness including Sylvia Plath's *The Bell Jar*, Doris Lessing's *The Summer Before the Dark*, and not only Virginia Woolf's novels but her life as well. As concerns Woolf, post-Laingian critics Roger Poole and Stephen Trombley have read Woolf's breakdown as stemming from her sense of being misunderstood and of the repression of her world view. They interpret her mental illness as the product of an insensitive incarceration enforced by her husband in league with her doctors. This reading of Woolf's *life* is aligned with the "male repression of female expression" reading of "The Yellow Wall-paper."

Gilman's narrative and Poole and Trombley's work on Woolf bring to the fore nineteenth- and early twentieth-century ideas concerning women's psychology. Woolf's own doctors wrote extensively about mental illness as an effect of moral deprivation which was then transmitted genealogically as well as about the importance of context on contraction and treatment of mental illness. G. H. Savage, one of Woolf's doctors, also provides a topical link between women's intellectual development and some kind of inevitable insanity and imbalance. This was fueled by the fear of the intellectual powers and possibilities of the New Woman, perceived as a threat to male power. While the British medical journal, *The Lancet*, produced text about women damaging their physical beings and specifically their reproductivity through book learning (thus depriving the world of generations of intelligent and successful males), Savage links study in general (which would include writing and intellectual pursuits) with mental illness in women:

> A strong and healthy girl of a nervous family is encouraged to read for examinations, and having distinguished herself, is, perhaps, sent to some fashionable forcing house where useless book learning is crammed into her. She is exposed, like the Strasbourgh geese, to stuffing of mental food in overheated rooms, and disorder of function results. Or if a similarly promising girl is allowed to educate herself at home, the danger of solitary work and want of social friction may be seen in conceit developing into insanity. (*Insanity and Allied Neuroses*, 23)

Faced with attitudes toward women's psychology such as these that link thinking and mental exertion with madness, Gilman's narrator in "The Yellow Wall-paper" is rendered powerless. She disagrees with her husband/doctor's prognosis but is in no position to contradict him. She cannot be heard:

> And what can one do?
>
> If a physician of high standing, and one's own husband, assures friends and relatives that there is really nothing the matter with one but temporary nervous depression—a slight hysterical tendency—what is one to do?
>
> [. . .]
>
> Personally, I believe that congenial work, with excitement and change, would do me good.
>
> But what is one to do? (29)

"The Yellow Wall-paper" explores how women's constraints under patriarchy lead to silencing and disempowerment and the ways in which any resistance to this oppression was read as "hysterical." Gilman's text articulates the suffering of one woman, and, in doing so, enables readers to appreciate the damage done by such controls and labels.

Read in the context of a medical profession which links madness with gender, prescribes stasis and loneliness to cure mental illness, and finds women who read, write, or study both threatening and sick, psychoanalytic and therapeutic readings emerge. Additionally, Gilman's text encourages an autobiographical reading, because the work itself sprang from her personal experience of depression and the rest cure prescribed by S. Weir Mitchell in 1887. Famously, Gilman was told by Mitchell to go home, restrict her reading to two hours a day, and, like her protagonist, to give up writing. Gilman notes, "I went home and obeyed the direction for three months, and came so near to the borderline of utter mental ruin that I could see over" (qtd. in Showalter 41). She recovered through ignoring the specialist's advice and getting back to work, which can be seen as a form of "writing through" her illness and out the other end. Gilman claims to have sent a copy of "The Yellow Wall-paper" to Mitchell and, although he did not respond to her, reports that, "many years later I was told that a great specialist had admitted to friends of his, that he had altered his treatment of neurasthenia since reading 'The Yellow Wall-paper'" (qtd. in Showalter 41).

Gilman can be seen as having broken down and then as having broken through; she saw over the borderline of mental ruin and wrote herself out of that state. But this is not always the solution nor even an option that all women (and men) have when facing breakdown. The breakdown equals breakthrough reading troubled me and my students in relation to those we knew suffering depression, breakdown, and schizophrenia. Exploring the origins of the "breakdown equals breakthrough" reading, my students' and my own discomfort with it, and considering what could lie beyond it, formed much of the experience of seminars spent on Gilman's text.

As I have begun to outline, an accepted feminist reading of "The Yellow Wall-paper" is that the narrator's breakdown at the end of the story is an expression of her rejection of the constraints of conventional women's roles; from this perspective, her breakdown is a subversive, positive move against repression and silencing. Gilbert and Gubar, for instance, see the narrator as "mad" in terms of society's standards but actually empowered. Kennard sees her madness as leading to a higher form of sanity or truth. Loralee MacPike and Beate Schöpp-Schilling see her madness as a creative and successful defiance.

This breakdown equals breakthrough reading derives in part from R. D. Laing's anti-psychiatry developed in the 1960s and '70s. Laing, along with Thomas Szasz, David Cooper, and Michel Foucault, developed the anti-psychiatry movement (although Laing rejected the label), which saw psychiatry as a form of social control, insanity and schizophrenia as often socially produced, and breakdown as often a way to break through stifling social conventions. Laing's phenomenological approach enabled people to see the world we perceive and ourselves within it as social constructs. He noted the social origins of so-called mental illness as opposed to the biochemical and did not believe that conventional psychiatry, including ECT, lobotomies, and incarcerations in psychiatric hospitals, provided answers for mental illness.

However, post-Laingian readers who have either experienced depression and breakdown or nursed and treated others who have gone through such experiences are sometimes very sceptical of interpretations of mental illness that view it as a positive response to "insane" social rules and conventions. As concerns representations of madness in women, such readers, students, critics, and academics argue that embracing a version of breakdown as liberating and empowering only serves to return women to the margins, the "locked room in the attic," and reifies stereotyped images of women as hysterical, indulged, and disempowered. From this perspective, a reading of "The Yellow Wall-paper" in which the narrator's breakdown is considered as a type of breakthrough is a dangerous trap that suggests no way forward. It sells women's experiences of social and personal alienation short; it refuses to recognize the medical, treatable causes of some depression and breakdown to the detriment of the sufferer, and it infantilizes women who articulate arguments against being silenced and figured as "Other," abject, dangerous, or strange. Readings which applaud breakdown as breakthrough ultimately disempower those who suffer the breakdowns rather than causing constructive and positive change in relationships and treatment. For many of my students, first-hand experience fueled doubts about Laingian-influenced readings which suggest that insanity or mental illness is always socially produced and that recognizing their social causes could empower the sufferer to use breakdown as a step to new insights, placing positive change in the hands of the sufferer. In their experiences, this perspective could be limiting, disabling, guilt-producing, and possibly dangerous.

In contrast to the breakdown equals breakthrough position, a medical or therapeutic reading enables students to consider "hysterical" representations of women as destructive and repressive. It also enables the consideration of some of the dangers of valuing breakdown as always leading to breakthrough when, in many instances, this is a misunderstanding of the personal suffering involved in depression, postnatal depression, and other forms of mental illness.

A dialogic pedagogical approach allows both the breakdown equals breakthrough and the medical/therapeutic approaches to Gilman's text to be introduced and involves students in contributing their own readings to this debate. Such a format-privileging dialogue and debate empowers students to articulate their interpretations and criticisms of other positions, while encouraging them to recognize that other interpretations may also hold validity. It enables them to speak out through the "cracks" and fissures in their perceptions of authorized readings and establish their own positions.

Teaching the Text: Mediating Between Approaches and Readings

Faced with (1) feminist readings of "breakdown equals breakthrough" in the face of patriarchal oppression; (2) post-Laingian views that depicting women's madness as a key to their gaining a voice is a sell-out that infantilizes women and leaves them in their breakdowns (waiting for breakthroughs); and (3) challenges by students with personal and professional experience, a dialogic approach to teaching the text seems essential. Students need to negotiate their reading through these contradictory and enlightening interpretations.

In the "Gender, Sexuality and Writing" third-year English literature module at Anglia Polytechnic University (APU), we began with Foucault and concentrated on how much nineteenth-century and early twentieth-century writing can be seen as a coding, questioning, and expression of positions—often resistant positions—on issues of sexuality and identity. Our reading of "The Yellow Wall-paper" produced a medley of responses. My previous experience had been that younger groups or more homogenous groups of adults felt shocked by the breakdown at the end of Gilman's text and responded positively to the feminist reading that breakdown leads to breakthrough. But my 1999 group broke out into major disagreements. A reasonable proportion of the group were mature women students, several of whom had medical backgrounds as nurses. Others had backgrounds which included depression or living with others who had gone through depression. For just a few, coming to the university to study was itself a breakthrough from depression, incarceration in the home, low-paid jobs, or full-time jobs as nurses. Several were still nursing as agency staff at nights and weekends. Issues represented in Gilman's text therefore were close to their experiences. They wanted, it seemed, to see Gilman's narrator's experience as enabling, to see angst leading to the expression of a liberated self. But they found that their own experiences constantly prevented this established feminist reading.

In order to negotiate these competing readings and to allow students to introduce their opinions and experiences, I introduced a dialogic approach to the text, making use of individual writing, small-group discussion, and large-group discussion. This approach focused on experiences of and treatments for depression as well as the question of whether breakdown can be considered a form of breakthrough.

Running a Dialogic Session on "The Yellow Wall-paper"

To open up a dialogic reading, i.e., one that holds oppositional readings in productive tension, I involve students in (1) small group discussion (2) large group discussion and debate, and (3) individual writing using responses made by other students as a basis for the development of their own critical responses.

Group discussion—with set questions that open up different readings—enables students to engage their own readings through extracts from the text. Since the questions are designed not to polarize response but are phrased in terms such as "how far is it fair to say—" and "in what way—," students are able to articulate divergent views and, in a best case scenario, simultaneously to hold opposing views, that is, to engage in dialogic reading that reads the text in several ways.

Writing responses individually enables articulation that could otherwise be silenced in a large discussion and enables students to go through the very motions that Gilman went through herself. By "writing their responses through," students learn that reading can be a debate between several different approaches.

It is important that these different readings be seen as a product of the dialogic nature of the text itself and of the text in dialogue with our lives as readers. The text can provoke different readings and arguments and that is its strength. One interpretation should not shut off others. Gilman's text makes us wonder about what "madness" is; how, if, and whether we can "write through" it to breakthrough; whether madness is always and only a social product or if it can be physiological as well; and whether, to some extent, the chance to speak out and articulate one's thoughts and feelings is a real answer to mental illness.

Session One Plan

I begin by giving students questions and extracts from the work of previous students. They are asked to consider the questions in light of the extracts and their own reading experiences. First, they work alone, and then the class is organized into small groups for discussion. At this later point, the students reflect on the variety of readings and the ways in which such readings help them to "touch base" with their own lives. Finally, they are asked to write their own responses to the text. I have provided sample student extracts below. Students whose responses are used here as *stimulus* material said that writing helped them to come to terms both with contradictions felt in a classroom where feminist readings seemed privileged over other medical/therapeutic readings and with the reactions the text produced in them personally. Having students share responses in small groups enables each student to engage personally with the text without having to come to a final agreed-upon reading with the rest of the class. It also enables them to share some personal feelings and experiences within the safety of a small group rather than in the relatively staged performance of the large group.

Questions to Students to Produce Reflective Writing and Food for Group Discussion

I provide the questions below with the following instruction: "Please consider the following personal, critical responses to the text. To what extent do they relate to your own responses?"

We have considered a variety of approaches to the text in this course. These have included:

- Feminist readings
- Medical/therapeutic readings
- Autobiographical readings
- Deconstructive readings
- Psychoanalytic readings
- Readings sympathetic to the husband

Can you now produce your own reflective reading, integrating personal experience and critical response? Write a short log of your responses to the text, negotiating among the various readings we have considered.

Extracts from Students' Work to Use as Stimuli for Discussion and Individual Responses

I provide students with the following extracts and the following question:

Question: How can these student readings inform your own? Use them to feed into your own reflective writing. Then discuss with your group how your own writing about the text negotiates your way through these various readings and the feminist reading supplied by the instructor.

1. This is a great piece of writing. Interesting because at this time in history postpartum depression has been recognized (or is it construed?) as an illness. The radical aspects of this story interest me because I have a nursing background, am also studying sociology, and have little choice academically but to see medical discourse as part and parcel of a patriarchal set-up. For me there is a conflict between the "caring professions" and what doctors and nurses believe they are doing, and the historic domination of men in the medical profession, and Foucault's "chemical gaze" theory, where deviance of any kind is defined depending on how things are seen in society at any one time. The fact that the author has some experience of this alienation from her society and her female role and the fact that I have been in contact with people who believe so strongly in such things as seeing things in wallpaper do make you question reality.
2. I thought it was really powerful. I had sympathy with the woman but realized her view of her husband was colored by her illness—deteriorating mental state. As a mother, I suppose I could understand her confused mental state post-childbirth. I saw the ending as the woman going "over the edge" into complete madness but not as her suicide. I think the language and sentence structure could be examined in more detail, as its pattern is revelatory regarding her deteriorating mental state.
3. My mother has had a breakdown. From my position I could identify with the main character as I had heard similar thoughts before. It educated me, as I was the onlooker to my own mother's stability reducing, as to how my mother may have felt. Coincidentally, she, too, banished herself into her bedroom! I homed in on the "madness" of the main character, questioning whether it really is insanity or whether she began seeing things as they really were.
4. Since I do suffer myself from manic depression, and since throughout the piece the narrator becomes increasingly ill with no indication as to her real state of mind at the beginning, I am aware that as a narrator she could be

thought to have a biased opinion of those looking after her, including her husband. That is not to say she did not believe what she said to be true, or that it was not true, merely that her thoughts and feelings may not have been based in reality.

5. Positive: overwrought description of a woman responding to repressive social conditions.
   Madness entirely sensible (preferable) reaction to intolerable situation, i.e., repressive society, no "space," oppressive home life.
   Difficulties: Distressing to read *because* of accuracy.
   Background: Coming from: two mental breakdowns, unable to accept social and personal implications of marriage and professional life within patriarchal world of business.

   As a result complete empathy with character in YW.

   Could be taught: As an escape narrative. I initially read this text as a positive reaction to an intolerable situation. The escape of the narrator into madness could be allied to the *Thelma and Louise* leap into an as-yet-uninvented space, a society that "works," has space for women.
6. "The Yellow Wall-paper" should not, I feel, be read as an attack against patriarchy. The speaker opens with an indirect attack—that the house is an ancestral hall, a hereditary estate—male line—then she goes on to be trapped in the house. The speaker's tone is unreliable in places. We should not necessarily be made to think that the husband is a villain. Perhaps he is a man traumatized by his wife's behavior—and a new baby! We only have her view—and she is severely depressed and may therefore be unreliable. Difficulties—some aspects of medicine still do not recognize postnatal depression—or antenatal. Important to remember historical context. Excellent piece of writing about a woman's feelings and emotions. An expression that emerges from deprivation. This piece written today would probably turn out similar, as the treatment for women in this predicament has changed very little.
7. The husband's attitude as a controlling figure also combining authority as a medical man and the effect this produces on his wife. He cares about her and wants to protect her. But he is as stuck in the right/acceptable ways of doing this as she is. The woman's only way of escape from an intolerable situation is through madness/complete breakdown. Practical solutions to problems that require radical re-thinking. Background: Sixties/seventies feminist thinking that men are the cause of society's problems!

Session Two Plan

What follows is an outline of how to use therapeutic/medical writings produced by students from both of my previous groups in a *debate*, a format I also use when teaching other texts. Divide students into two groups, one arguing for the validity of therapeutic/medical reading (breakdown is destructive) and one for the feminist "breakdown equals breakthrough" reading of the text (other positions could be assigned as well). Initially, I divide the class into four groups—two for the medical/therapeutic side, two for the feminist breakdown equals breakthrough side. Each group decides on its main points, discusses the text, and then combines with the other group also defending the same position. When the two groups combine, some sharing of readings takes place, as does some allocation of roles and questions, arguments, responses, bits of text, critical points, etc.

Debate Guidelines

- Everyone must contribute.
- The session is chaired.
- Each large group has a speaker and a seconder.

Part way through the debate, there is a pause when each group reconvenes briefly to decide how to sum up, to bring in those group members who have not raised their point yet, and to make responses to the other group's points. By the end, although a vote may be taken over which "side" or reading wins, it is clearly put to the students that choices over critical readings depend quite often upon who produces the readings, how forcibly they argue, and how topical that kind of critical approach is at the time of the argument—in short, that both readings and their acceptance are culturally produced.

Group Discussion Questions

One way to stimulate small group discussion is to ask groups to assess student writings. Provided below are two medical/therapeutic responses from students to the text. I provide students with such responses and ask them to consider the following questions: "How does the medical/therapeutic reading of 'The Yellow Wall-paper' open up for us engagements with it as a text which imaginatively and realistically represents women's breakdown, postnatal depression, and psychotic states? What implications does this understanding of the medical/therapeutic reading have for you and your reading of the text?

Medical/Therapeutic Readings

Student Liz Burns

Depression associated with female biology—menstruation, child-bearing, etc.—is still stigmatized (of course, this is a generalization and does not apply in all cases by any means), and the sufferers are made to bear a burden of guilt and responsibility for their own difficulties, not only by professionals but by their nearest and dearest. The social pressures which preserve this state of affairs, more than a quarter of a century after Brown and Harris (1978, *Social Origins of Depression*) successfully argued the paramount importance of social factors in the development of depression, are powerful and intimately connected with the relationship of men and women in society. This state of affairs is very clearly set out, more or less in these terms, in "The Yellow Wallpaper," and it is shocking to realize that this text is over 110 years old.

For me, as a family therapist, this story is most compelling in its portrayal of the way in which individual psychopathology fits with the communications and relationship ties of family intimacy. The mixture of concern, authority/ownership, and affection shown by John, the doctor, to his nameless wife, is potent in keeping her in her place and reinforcing the status quo. She is responsible, in that the problem is seen to reside in her, yet she is forbidden to take any kind of action to help herself, and her thoughts and opinions are defined as "sick" and therefore have no status. This kind of communication, especially in the context of unequal power, is the kind of thing we recognize as creating an impossible "bind" within which the relatively powerless (children, the sick and disabled, people, particularly women from ethnic minorities) are easily imprisoned. Systemic thinking would also suggest a reciprocity here, so that the oppressors and the oppressed are both stuck together (though maybe unequally) in a vicious circle of disempowering communication.

I wonder if professional readers might be encouraged to note that the story creates the sense of endless, and ultimately futile, reflection (though not self-reflection). This is rather similar to perseveration, or the constant round of unproductive thoughts, which might be part of a psychotic process.

This text lends itself very well to thinking about the reading process itself and how this may be similar/different from the process of listening to patients/clients and making sense of what they say in order to frame a course of action (diagnosis, treatment plan, etc). The story dwells on the shape of the wallpaper design, its color, and the way in which the narrator interprets these characteristics as active, oppressive, unhealthy, malign but also intimately connected to herself and her own state of mind.

Student Andrea Watson

From the very beginning of this short story, one is confronted with a very common scenario—perhaps only marginally less common now than when this story was written. That is, the communications of someone in a troubled internal state of mind are received and reacted to on a conscious rational level only, i.e., that if there is no obvious external reason for the disturbance, then it can be dealt with by the application of common sense and sensible explanation. In this way the communications of the "mad" person are not only not ascribed meaning, they are steadily robbed of it. This may or may not accelerate the descent into madness but certainly would offer very little comfort or containment. Reading this story, however, from a psychoanalytic perspective, with the idea that the internal world, the world of the imagination and of unconscious processes, is just as real as the external world, can take one in very interesting directions. I think one can take the room with the yellow wallpaper to stand as a metaphor for the narrator's own mind. She is a woman whom we hear, almost in passing, has recently had a baby boy and yet she says: "I can not be with him, it makes me so nervous" (31). Immediately the possibility of a postnatal disturbance presents itself, that what makes her so nervous about the baby are the thoughts that have been stirred up in her mind by the experience of pregnancy and birth. These thoughts are hinted at in the first description of the nursery—note that it was originally a nursery—with its windows barred.

She does not want to be in this room. She begs her husband to allow her to stay in another room—she feels that the room evokes thoughts and ideas that she hates. We have references to suicide in the above passage and later there is reference to murder: "There is a recurrent spot where the pattern lolls like a broken neck and two bulbous eyes stare at you upside down" (32). In postnatal psychosis, the baby often has projected into it some of the mother's very frightened and frightening ideas and thoughts, and the baby is felt to be in danger from them: "If we had not used it, that blessed child would have! [. . .] Why, I wouldn't have a child of mine [. . .] live in such a room for worlds" (35). She does not feel that the baby has a safe place in this room/mind.

Gradually as the story unfolds, we see the dividing line in her mind that is represented by the wallpaper itself between fact and fantasy, dream and reality, sanity and madness begin to disintegrate. The mad part of her self begins to dominate, and instead of now struggling against the convoluted ways of the wallpaper, she throws herself into them and invites the madness in.

Conclusion

These teaching and learning strategies enable dialogic readings and encourage medical/therapeutic, personal, and feminist critical responses. Additionally, by using differing forms of group work and students' own writings as stimuli for thought, discussion, writing, and debate, one deliberately can remove the authoritative reading of the teacher, included early on as one in a range of potential readings. Through these strategies, students can engage both with the text and readings of it, making meaning themselves, arguing for it beyond the personal, while recognizing the role that personal, experiential reading has in our appreciation of texts—particularly sensitive, engaging, and provocative texts such as "The Yellow Wall-paper."

Works Cited

Dock, Julie Bates, Comp. and Ed. *Charlotte Perkins Gilman's "The Yellow Wall-paper" and the History of Its Publication and Reception: A Critical Edition and Documentary Casebook.* University Park, PA: The Pennsylvania State University Press, 1998.

Foucault, Michel. *The History of Sexuality (Volume 1: An Introduction).* London: Penguin, 1978.

Gilbert, Sandra M., and Susan Gubar. *The Madwoman in the Attic: The Woman Writer and the Nineteenth-Century Literary Imagination.* New Haven: Yale University Press, 1979.

Gilman, Charlotte Perkins. "The Yellow Wallpaper." 1892. *Charlotte Perkins Gilman's "The Yellow Wall-paper and the History of Its Publication and Reception: A Critical Edition and Documentary Casebook.* Comp. and Ed. Julie Bates Dock. University Park, PA: The Pennsylvania State University Press, 1998. 29–42.

——. "Why I Wrote 'The Yellow Wallpaper.'" *The Charlotte Perkins Gilman Reader.* Ed. Ann J. Lane. New York: Pantheon Books, 1980. 19–20.

Hedges, Elaine. R. "'Out at Last?' "The Yellow Wall-paper" after Two Decades of Feminist Criticism." *Critical Essays on Charlotte Perkins Gilman.* Ed. Joanne B. Karpinski. New York: G. K. Hall, 1992. 222–33

Kennard, Jean E. "Convention Coverage or How to Read Your Own Life." *New Literary History* 13 (Autumn 1981): 69–88.

Laing, R. D. *The Politics of the Family and Other Essays.* New York: Vintage Books, 1972.

——. *The Facts of Life.* New York: Ballantine Books, 1976.

——. *The Politics of Experience.* New York: Ballantine Books, 1967.

——. *The Divided Self.* Harmondsworth: Penguin Books, 1965.

MacPike, Loralee, "Environment and Psychopathologial Symbolism in 'The Yellow Wallpaper'." *American Literary Realism 1870–1910* 8 (Summer 1975): 286–88.

Poole, Roger. *The Unknown Virginia Woolf.* London: Routledge, 1980.

Savage, G. H. *Insanity and Allied Neuroses.* London: Cassell, 1884.

Savage, G. H. "The Pathology of Insanity." *British Medical Journal* 2, 1884.

Schöpp-Schilling, Beate. "'The Yellow Wall-paper': A Rediscovered Realistic Story." *American Literary Realism 1870–1910* 8 (Summer 1975): 284–86.

Showalter, Elaine. *The Female Malady.* London: Virago, 1995.

Trombley, Stephen. *All That Summer She Was Mad.* London: Junction Books, 1981.

I thank Liz Burns, Andrea Watson, and the Gender Sexuality and Writing Seminar 1999 for their comments.

CONTRIBUTORS

Janet Gebhart Auten directs the Writing Center and teaches graduate student teachers in the Literature Department at American University in Washington, DC. Her published articles concern teaching nineteenth-century writers such as Jewett and Emerson. Her recent work on nineteenth-century women writers appears in a conference volume, *Gendered Landscapes: An Interdisciplinary Exploration of Past Place and Space* and in *"The Only Efficient Instrument": 19th Century Women Writers and the Periodical 1830–1914* (forthcoming).

Jonathan Crewe is Willard Professor of English and Comparative Literature and Director of the Humanities Center at Dartmouth College. Although he is a specialist in Renaissance literature, his oft-cited essay "Queering 'The Yellow Wallpaper'?: Charlotte Perkins Gilman and the Politics of Form" appeared in *Tulsa Studies in Women's Literature* in the fall of 1995, and his contribution to this collection expands upon that essay.

Joanne B. Karpinski is Associate Professor of English at Regis University in Denver and is a noted Gilman scholar. She is the editor of *Critical Essays on Charlotte Perkins Gilman* as well as *Frontier Gothic: Terror and Wonder in the American Wilderness.*

Jim O'Loughlin is a Visiting Assistant Professor at the University of Northern Iowa. He is co-author, with Julie Husband, of *Daily Life in the Industrial*

United States: 1870–1900 (forthcoming from Greenwood Press). He has published in *Modern Language Studies*, *Proteus*, *New Literary History*, and *Socialist Review*.

Debra K. Peterson is a doctoral candidate in English at Wayne State University with an interest in how spatial representations are utilized in electronic culture. She has employed "The Yellow Wall-paper" in a variety of classroom settings.

Marjean D. Purinton is Associate Professor of English and Women's Studies at Texas Tech University. She has published and spoken extensively on the subject of pedagogy and has two forthcoming essays on teaching romantic-period women poets and the gothic novel, respectively.

Paul Reifenheiser received his doctorate from Florida State University in August of 2001, where he is currently instructor of English. His dissertation "Specters of Apostasy: Charting the Postmodern Crossing of U.S. Literature and Religious Studies in the 1960s," focuses on the ways in which texts of the 1960s both chronicled and fueled the burgeoning religious shift from modernism to postmodernism.

Robyn Shaw teaches English at the Euro-American Institute and the ESPEME Business School in Nice, France. Her master's thesis focused on the intersections between existential philosophy and nineteenth-century literature.

Jeffrey Andrew Weinstock is assistant professor of English at Central Michigan University. With Sarah Higley, he is the co-editor of *Critical Approaches to the Blair Witch Project* (forthcoming, Wayne State University Press), and he has published on a variety of nineteenth-century American literary and contemporary popular culture topics.

Gina Wisker is co-coordinator for Women's Studies at Anglia Polytechnic University in Cambridge, UK, where she teaches English literature, and is Director of Learning and Teaching Development. Her publications include *Postcolonial and African American Women's Writing* (2000), *Virginia Woolf—A Beginner's Guide* (2000), *Sylvia Plath—A Beginner's Guide* (2001), and numerous essays on women's horror, postcolonial women's writing, Charlotte Mew, and Edith Sitwell. She is also co-editor of the journal *Innovations in Education and Teaching International*.

INDEX